Dear Customer

IMPORTANT — Please Read This Now !

We are delighted to announce a special free service for all of our customers.

Simply complete this form and return it to the FREEPOST address overleaf to receive:

A Free Customer Newsletter
B Free Information Service
C Exclusive Customer Offers - which have included free software, videos and relevant products
D Opportunity to take part in product development sessions
E The chance for you to write about your own business experience and become one of our respected autors

Fill this now and return it to us to join our customer information service.

Name : ______________________ Position : ______________________

Company/Organisation : ______________________

Address (including postcode) : ______________________

______________________ Country : ______________________

Telephone : ______________________ Fax : ______________________

Nature of business : ______________________

Title of book purchased : ______________________

ISBN (printed on back cover) : ☐☐☐☐ ☐☐☐☐☐ ☐

Comments : ______________________

— — — — — — — — — — — **Fold Here Then Staple Once** — — — — — — — — — — —

We would be very grateful if you could answer these questions to help us with market research

1. Where/How did you hear of this book?

☐ in a bookshop
☐ in a magazine/newspaper (please state which) :
____
☐ information through the post
☐ recommendation from a colleague
☐ other (please state which) :
____

2. Where did you buy this book

☐ Direct from Reliance Publishing House
☐ From a bookclub
☐ From a bookshop (state which)
____

3. Which newspaper(s)/magazine(s) do you read regularly? :

____
____

4 When buying a book which factors influence you most?
(Please rank in order)

☐ recommendation from a colleague
☐ price
☐ content
☐ recommendation in a bookshop
☐ author
☐ publisher
☐ title
☐ other(s) :
____

5 Is this book a

☐ personal purchase?
☐ company purchase?
☐ library purchase?

6 Would you be prepared to spend a few minutes talking to our customer services staff to help with product development?

YES/NO

We occasionally make our customer lists available to companies whose products or services we feel may be of interest. If you do not want this service write 'exclude from other mailings' on this card. The Customer Information Service is liable to change without notice.

JAINTIA HILLS – A MEGHALAYA TRIBE

ITS ENVIRONMENT, LAND AND PEOPLE

JAINTIA HILLS –
A MEGHALAYA TRIBE
ITS ENVIRONMENT, LAND AND PEOPLE

Editors :
Dr. P. M. Passah
Dr. S. Sarma

RELIANCE PUBLISHING HOUSE
NEW DELHI

First Published 2002

ISBN : 81-7510-152-0

Price : Rs. 295/- $ 57/-

Published by :
Dr. S. K. Bhatia
(Life Member ILA, FEPI, HWF, INSA, Common Cause, ISCKON)
Reliance Publishing House
3026/7H, Ranjit Nagar,
New Delhi-110008
Ph. : 5737377 / 5852605
Fax : 5786769

Composed by :
Elegant Printographics
74, Savera Apptt., Sector-13,
Plot-5, Rohini, Delhi-85
E-mail : akm_akm@yahoo.com

Printed by :
S.S.S. Printers
New Delhi.

CONTENTS

LIST OF FIGURES

LIST OF TABLES

PREFACE

This book, Jaintia Hills: - A Meghalaya Tribe

Its Environment, Land and People is dedicated to the memory of Late Professor Barrister Pakem, a former President of North East India Council for Social Science Research and a former Vice-Chancellor of North-Eastern Hill University.

From an obscure village of Jaintia Hills of Meghalaya emerged a person who was self made to shine as one of the brightest stars of Meghalaya. Professor Pakem rose from a humble beginning to the top of the academic eminence to have become the Vice Chancellor of North-Eastern Hill University, one of the Central Universities of the country. As a political scientist, he had the opportunity to show how a politician could be pragmatic and also a man of public ethics. His life and work are a great testimony to the fact that nothing is unachievable in life provided one has an iron will and a sincere aspiration. Money and wealth are not always the criteria as amply demonstrated by Barrister Pakem.

Professor Pakem was a man of varied and mixed qualities of head and heart. People all over the country who once met him appreciated his high calibre, moral character and integrity both in the academic and public life. He was an outstanding teacher, a political scientist and a liberal thinker. He was awarded the prestigious Pandit Jawaharlal Nehru Award in Social Science by Madhya Pradesh Council of Science and Technology in 1996 in recognition of his outstanding contribution to overall development studies in North East India. He was indeed one of the great sons of contemporary India. This scholar extraordinary displayed probity and rectitude in public affairs and represented values of the highest order in society.

This volume contains 23 articles by eminent social scientists and scientists belonging to agriculture, forestry, demography and life sciences. Scholars adopted a multi-disciplinary approach in their study of environment, land and people of Jaintia Hills on the international border with Bangladesh. The cultural influences are two-way traffic.

The Jaintia Hills eco-system is under heavy stress due to unscientific coal mining and systematic destruction of forest resources. The rich fertile lands are now exposed to forces of nature due to unplanned deforestation over the decades. The rich soil is now highly degraded. The unscientific opencast coal mining has caused wide-spread pollution of streams and rivers. The green valleys now look like deserted wild fields due to opencast mining. Nevertheless, the Jaintias are known for their zeal. They are waking up and there is new initiative and enterprise in reviving economic activities to realise the economic potentialities of the Jaintia Hills. The Papers in this volume are ample testimony of the economic, cultural and social life of the Jaintias.

The North-East India Council for Social Science Research held a commemorative seminar in honour of Professor Barrister Pakem on 5 and 6 June 2000. We are grateful to the Indian Council for Social Science Research, North Eastern Regional Centre and Ms. Neiniroi Khonglah-Pakem for giving us generous support to hold the seminar. We also thank Mr. E.K. Mawlong, Chief Minister of Meghalaya for inaugurating the Seminar. Mr. Mawlong was a colleague of Professor Pakem in social and political field. We take this opportunity to thank Dr. S.K. Bhatia, Proprietor of Reliance Publishing House for publishing this book expeditiously.

B. Datta Ray
Secretary
North East Council for Social Science Research

Shillong,
November 24, 2001

INTRODUCTION

P.M. Passah
S. Sarma

The North East India Council for Social Science Research, Shillong held a Commemorative Seminar on , 5 and 6 of June 2000 in honour of Professor Barrister Pakem on the theme Jaintia Hills: A Meghalaya Tribe: Environment, Land and People. Many scholars from different parts of the North Eastern Region and beyond, participated in the Seminar and 22 of them submitted their Papers on various aspects of the theme. The- economic development of Jaintia Hills needs to be focussed prominently and holding of the Seminar in honour of late Professor Pakem who loved Jaintia Hills to the core of his heart, is the right step that was taken by the Council in spite of financial constraint.

The district of Jaintia Hills lies between Latitudes 20°58' and 26°3'N and Longitudes 91°59' and 92°51'E and covers an area of 3295.5 sq. kms. approximately. It is surrounded on the north, the east and the south east by Assam; on the south by Bangladesh and on the west by Khasi Hills. It is populated mostly by the Jaintias or Syntengs with a small group of Biates and Hmars occupying the southeast corner of the district. The late Suniti Kumar Chatterjee; an international philologist must be correct in suggesting that the name Jaintia could be an Aryanized form of the name *Synteng* by which the people of Jaintia Hills used to be called even today. From the word *Synteng* we get *Syntein, Syntiang, Zontain, Zontia,* and ultimately "Jaintia". Again the name "Synteng" could also be an Aryanized form of the name "Sutong", the original clan of the Jaintia royal dynasty from which was also derived the names "Suteng" and "Sutnga".

It is very wrong to say that the name "Jaintia" has now been largely replaced by the term "Pnar".[1] In fact, the people residing in the central region of Jaintia Hills are called "Pnars" by those living in the southern and northern regions and who are in turn being called as "Wars" and "Bhois" respectively by the Pnars. But all the three are collectively known by a generic name "Jaintias" or "Syntengs".

The present day Jaintia Hills district is but a remnant of the erstwhile Jaintia Kingdom which had been subjected to repeated divisions and partitions since the advent of the British in the North Eastern region and immediately after India's Independence. The Jaintia state was one of the oldest states in the region (see accompanying Map). It was mentioned in the Puranic and Tantrik literature. Its genesis is very obscure but mythologies and legends help in gleaning some facts relating to its state formation. It was computed by scholars that U Chyngklein Am, the eldest son of Ka Li Dakha and U Luh Ryndi, ruled the Jaintia state in the 3rd Century B.C.[2]

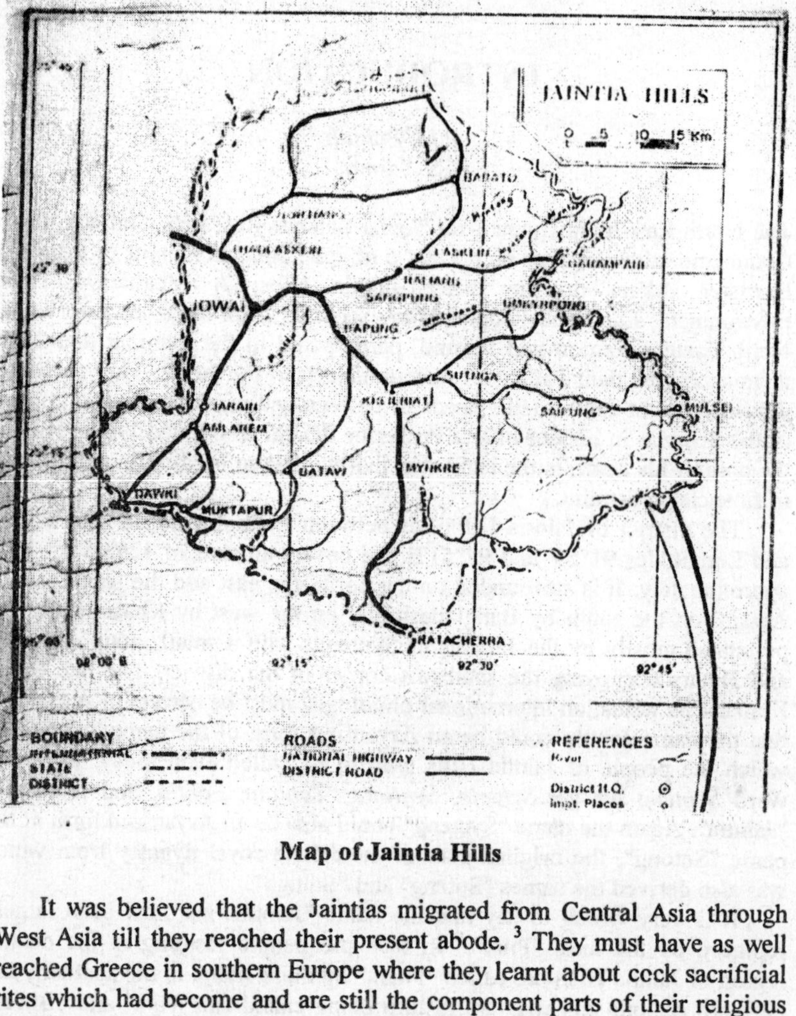

Map of Jaintia Hills

It was believed that the Jaintias migrated from Central Asia through West Asia till they reached their present abode. [3] They must have as well reached Greece in southern Europe where they learnt about cock sacrificial rites which had become and are still the component parts of their religious sacrifices." They might have also crossed over the Mediterranean Sea to North Africa where they learnt the art of erecting memorial and tomb stones. Jaintia Hills has one of the largest collections of ancient monoliths, menhirs and tomb stones. They returned to `West Asia where they imbibed knowledge about sheep and goat sacrifices.' They proceeded eastward till they reached North India thence along the Terai region of the Himalayas they moved on to North Burma where they turned southwards to South-East Asia. They turned round and moved back northwards across Burma till they reached the impenetrable forest areas of the present-day Jaintia Hills. [4] It was further believed that the main body, however, moved on into the Gangetic Plain, when Aryan penetration drove them into the hills of Central and Eastern India. Hence their descendants are met with today as speakers of the Munda languages.[5]

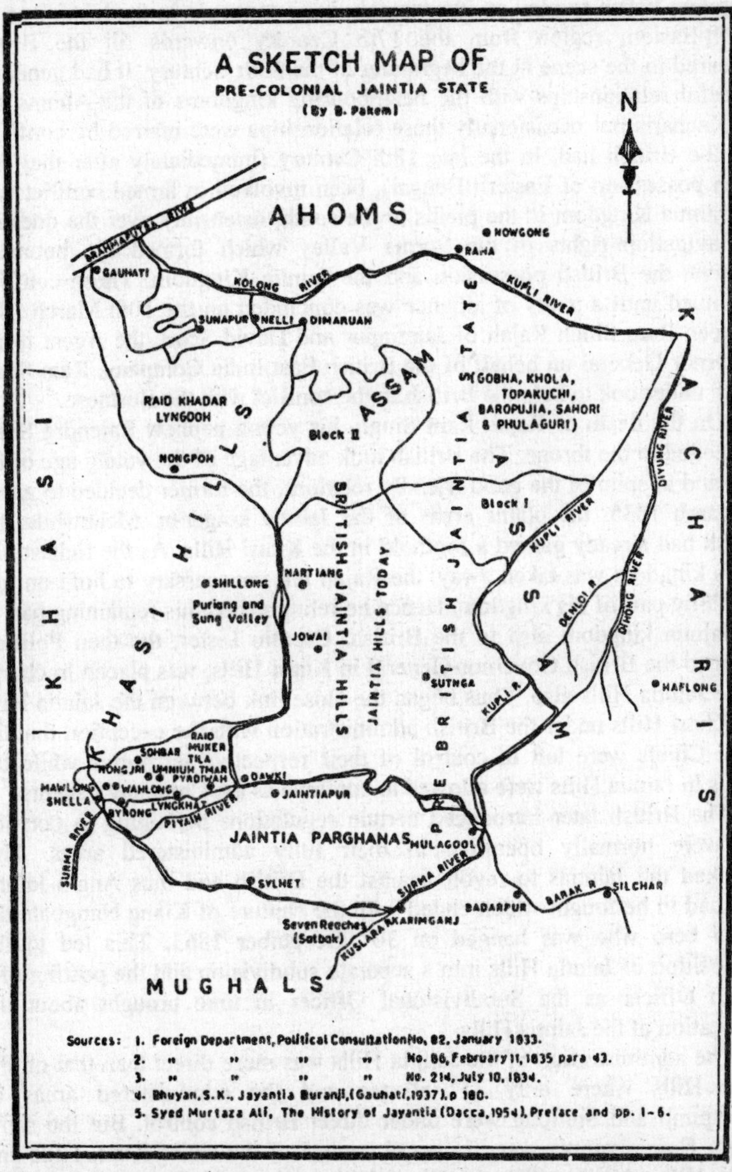

Source: B. Pakem, "State Formation in Pre-Colonial Jaintia" in Surajit Sinha (Ed.) *Tribal Politics and State System in Pre-Colonial Eastern and North Eastern India*, (K.P. Bagchi & Co., Calcutta – Delhi), 1987

A Sketch Map of Pre-colonial Jaintia State

It is true that the present Jaintia Hills district constituted the nucleus from which the erstwhile Jaintia Kingdom eventually emerged. The Kingdom began to play an increasingly important role in the history of the North-Eastern region from the 17th Century onwards till the British appeared in the scene at the beginning of the 19th Century. It had generally peaceful relationships with the neighbouring kingdoms of the Ahoms and the Kacharis but occasionally these relationships were marred by conflicts. But the British had, in the late 18th Century (immediately after they had taken possession of Eastern Bengal), been involved in armed conflict with the Jaintia Kingdom in the plains to the south, ostensibly over the question of navigation rights in the Surma Valley which formed the boundary between the British possession and the Jaintia Kingdom. These conflicts continued until a treaty of alliance was concluded on the 10th March 1824 between Ram Singh Rajah of Jaintiapur and David Scott, the Agent to the Governor General on behalf of the British East India Company. Ram Singh Rajah undertook to help the British in the conflict with the Burmese.[6]

On the death of Rajah Ram Singh, his young nephew Rajendra Singh succeeded to the throne. The British took advantage of the young age of the king and in spite of the good friendly relations, the former decided to annex in March 1835, the plains areas of the Jaintia kingdom. Meanwhile, the British had already gained a foothold in the Khasi Hills. As the richest part of his kingdom was taken away, the Rajah felt unnecessary to hold on to a poor hilly part of his kingdom. Hence he relinguished this remaining part of the Jaintia kingdom also to the British. Captain Lister, the then Political Agent to the British Governor-General in Khasi Hills; was placed in charge of the Jaintia Hills also. Thus began the close link between the Jaintia Hills and Khasi Hills under the British administration with the exception that the Khasi Chiefs were left in control of their respective territories while the Dolois in Jaintia Hills were allowed to continue as the Company's agents.[7]

The British later introduced certain regulations pertaining to taxation that were normally operative in their fully administered areas. This provoked the Jaintias to revolt against the British and thus Anglo-Jaintia wars had to be fought which ended with the capture of Kiang Nangbah, the Jaintia hero who was hanged on 30th December 1863. This led to the composition of Jaintia Hills into a separate subdivision and the posting of a British Officer as the Subdivisional Officer in time brought about the pacification of the Jaintia Hills.[8]

The administration of the Jaintia Hills was more direct than that on the Khasi Hills where only 31 villages and the administered areas of Cherrapunji and Shillong were under direct British control. But the same Deputy Commissioner was in overall control of the entire Khasi Hills and Jaintia Hills. Again unlike the Khasi Hills, the whole of Jaintia Hills was enfranchised under the Government of India Act 1835 and elected its own representative to the Assam Legislative Assembly.[9] The adoption of the Sixth Schedule a to the Constitution of India in 1950 saw the creation of one district council known as the United Khasi-Jaintia Hills Autonomous District Council. But in 1964 a separate district council for the Jaintia Hills was created and after the new State of Meghalaya was carved out of Assam in 1972, the new District of Jaintia Hills was also created immediately in the same year.

During the last 28 years, much had been invested through plan allocation for the socio-economic development of the district. But the State has much still to do to build and raise the capability of the people and the district itself. The infrastructure development in the district is still too weak to sustain any vigorous programme for its economic development. There are still serious bottlenecks particularly in the fields of inter-state transport, power, entrepreneurial manpower and technical manpower and in the field of social services like health and education. Thus both the human capability and the capability of the district have to be strongly built and raised to the level that can properly exploit and utilize the rich natural resources of the district for the economic welfare of the people.

REFERENCES

1. I.M. Simon (ed.) (1996), Government of Meghalaya, Arts and Culture Department, Shillong, Gazetteer of India; Meghalaya District Gazetteer; Jaintia Hills District, p.1.
2. B. Pakem, "State Formation in Pre-Colonial Jaintia" in Surajit Sinha, (1987), (ed.), *Tribal Politics and State Systems in Pre-Colonial Eastern and North Eastern India* (K.P. Bagchi & Company, Calcutta), pp.243-5.
3. *Ibid*
4. *Ibid*
5. G.E. Hall, *A History of South East Asia*, p.221.
6. *Meghalaya District Gazetteer*, op. cit., pp.1-2.
7. *Ibid*
8. *Ibid*
9. *Ibid*

1

ENVIRONMENT, LAND AND PEOPLE OF JAINTIA HILLS

N N Bhattacharyya

INTRODUCTION

The Jaintia Hills is the eastern part of the Meghalaya Plateau abode of clouds named by Professor S.P.Chatterjee in 1932. This plateau studied in detail by him and published in the name and style as Le Plateau de Meghalaya in 1936, Paris. Geologically the whole Meghalaya plateau including the Karbi Anglong region of Assam is a detached part of the Reminsular India. It is separated by the Malda gap which resulted of river erosion of the Ganga and the Brahmaputra.[1] Thus the landscape evolution of the plateau is closely linked with the Indian deminsula and its landscape story consists of different types of erosien, sedimentation, folding, intrusions, movements of land and sea and emissions. The core of the plateau is an ancient mass of gneiss, schists and granite which have been exposed in the north but hidden in the south beneath cretaceous and Tertiary depositis and a Mesozoic trap known as sylhet traps. The whole plateau was under sub-aerial erosion from the cambrian to the Jurassic period. It centains within its face the marks peneplaination which ranges from pre-cambrian to recent and sub-recent periods. The peneplains are at varying altitudes of 1860- 1920 m around Shillong, Latkor peaks 1440-1500m and 1410 m in Unkhrah val1ey.

ENVIRONMENT AND LAND :

The Jaintia Hills forms a oontiguous part of the Khasi Hills consisting of northern undulating hills, Jowai upland and the southern escarpment. There are more flat lands in the Jaintia Hills than that of the Khasi Hills. The general height of the district is in between 1250 metres and 1750 metres. The Jowai upland acts as a water shed between the Brahmaputra valley and the Surma Valley.

The central part of the study area is mainly constituted by the rocks of the pre-cambrian age. The pre-Tertiary and Tertiary rocks occur above these rocks which form the basement for the younger formation. The Jaintia series of rocks is predominently composed of sandstones with clay, coal seams and fossiliferous limestones. These are all Tertiary formations and belong to the shelf facies. The Jaintia series can be geologically sub-divided into three stages, namely Kopili stage, Sylhet Limestone stage and Theria stage.

The Jaintia Hills is formed of various rock types with varying lithological characters. Different agents of denudation like rainfall, surface water and temperature conditions have played an important role on the rock types in moulding the landforms of the area.

The climate of Meghalaya differs from the plains of North East India mainly due to its elevation. At the foot hills of the plateau the climate is humid and warm. The central upland experiences very cold night during the winter where the temperature goes down to 1.7°c. The temperature never rises above 26°c in any part of the year. But there is a great variation of reinfall in the plateau from south to north due to a rain shadow effect on the areas lying to the north. For example, Cherrapunji which is located on the high ridge has a rainfall over 1200 cm, while Shillong being located 50 km to the north of it gets only 230 cm. The average minimum rainfall is 251 em and maximum is 367 at Jowai and this station does not experiences any rainshadow effect. Because of high rainfall the top soils in the upland is very thin and in some places rocks like grainte, slate, limestone, sandstone, coal etc. lie bare in patches. The major parts of the Jaintia Hills consists of red loamy soil, red yellow soil and laterite soil. These soils are usually acidic, rich in organic matter and nitrogen but deficient phosphate and Potash. Such soils are good for the cultivation of fruits. potatoes, arecanut, betelvine and hill rice in hill slopes and teraces. Depending on rainfall and altitude, the Jaintia Hills is clad with varieties of tropical and temperate vegetations. These can be divided into three types : mixed evergreen forests, grass lands and pine forests. The mixed evergreen type consists of many broad leafed trees and shrubs with scattered bamboos, timber trees like Shorea robusta, Shorea assamica vatica lanceofolia, Tetrameles nudiflora, Mesua ferea etc. All these vegetation predominate the hill slopes of the lower part in the district. Plants like banana, Araceae, Marantaceae herbs grow on the valley bottoms and water plants like Monochoria, Ottelia, Vallisneria and Salvinia etc. are found in the broad sluggish streams. The hill tops with shallow subsoil support grasses and herbs like Gentians, Swertia, Osbeckia and Lamiaceae herbs. Temperate vegetation like pinus insularis, Elaeocarpus, Manglietia Sp. etc are predominent in the Jowai upland. Besides, there are sacred groves in the district. The dominating plants of such groves are Rhododendren arborea and Quercus Spp., Broad leafed trees like Cinnamomum, Bucklandia, Carpinus Schima etc. are also found in different sacred groves of the Jaintia Hills. In the coal mining areas are now devoid of trees and scrubs. The unscientific mining of coal in the Jaintia Hills has caused deforestation besides other problems of soil erosion, water and air pollution and general environmental degradation.

PEOPLE OF JAINTIA HILLS

The original residents of the Jaintia Hills were known as Syntengs and later they became Jaintias. Acctarding to historians the ancient Jaintias were immigrants somewhere from the Cambodian region and from the banks of the Mekong river. They came into ancient Assam via Patkoi range and finally occupied the Jaintia Hills. The Jaintias seem to have been an Aryanization of the original Austric word synteng which developed into Jaintia. The exact date of arrival of the Jaintias and Khasis is very much uncertain. Some neolithic findings tell that they belong to an antifiated race.

Generally the Jaintias are known as Syntengs but they prefer to be called Pnars. They are inhabitants of the Jaintia Hills. The war Syntengs are concentrated in the south of the Jaintia Hills. Besides, Mikirs (Karbies) Lalungs (Tiwas), Hadems, Kholtangs. Khelmas etc and nontribals are inhabiting in different parts of the Jaintia Hills.

It is said that at one period the whole Meghalaya state formed one kingdom which comprised both hill and plain of Assam and Bangladesh. Then it became spiltup into two kingdoms, namely Jaintia and Khyrim. The whole of Jaintia Hills including the adjacent plains was ruled by Sutnga Syiems. Lying in the southeast of Jowai town Sutnga served as the political headquarters of Sutnga Syiems during the early times. One of the kings of Sutnga was tempted to invade and anex Jaintiapur to his kingdom in the medieval period. It was perhaps during the region of U Pyrvat Roy, Sutnga Kingdom was extended to Jaintiapur, a plainland south of the Jaintia Hills which became a part of the Sutnga Syiemship in about 1500 A.D. Sir Edward Gait also made a remark: "The dominions of the Rajahs of Jaintia included two entirely distincts tracts of country, namely the Jaintia Hills, which are inhabited by a Khasi tribe called Synteng and the plain country. South of these Hills and North of the Barak River, in the Sylhet District now known as the Jaintia Parganahs, the inhabitants of which are the Bengalee Hindus and Muhammadans. The former tract was the original home of the dynasty. The latter was a later annexation, but it was the area which bore the name of Jaintia and which is mentioned in Pauranik and Tantrik literature as containing one of the 51 famous shrines sacred to Durga"2. Sutnga Syiems adopted Hindu names and symbols, observing tantrik rites at the Shrine of goddess. The Jaintias have no recorded history of their own like the Khasis till the advent of the British. During the British period the British administrators considered both the Jaintias and the Khasis as one tribe. But some ritual events like the Behdienkhlam festival among the Jaintias play a very important role in enhancing separate ethnic identity. Prior to 1826 the whole of Jaintia Hills formed a single Syiemship which was split into 12 administrative units called the Doloiships is its internal Political organisation. In 1835 the Jaintia Syiemship lapsed and the whole of Jaintia Hills including the Brahmaputra and the Surma valley became an integral part of the company's territory.

The Jaintias speak the language of the Mon-Khmer origin which belongs to the Austro-Asiatic linguistic groun. The important feature of this linguistic group is monosyllabic in form. The Jaintias had only one religion narned Niamtre earlier in which beefeating was prohibited. Perhaps they shared Hindu beliefs in showing reverance to a cow. During the British period a large section of Jaintias became christian and at present they have two religious groups, namely Niamtre (trarditional) and Christian. The traditioinal rites and ritual performances of Niamtres are resembling Hinduism. The Jaintias belong to matrilineal society and their social, cultural and economic set up is based on matrilineal and matrilocal traits.

The total area of the Jaintia Hills is 3819 Sq.Km. with a population of 2,20,473 (1991). Out of these 119872 persons live in 459 villages and 20601 persons live in only urban centre i.e. Jowai. The general density of population was 58 per sq.km. in the year 1991 which was quite high because of hilly nature of the tenain with primary sector of economy comprising agriculture forest and coal mining. The sex ratio of the district was 973 which was higher than that of Meghalaya (955) and the country as a whole (929) as per 1991 census. The literacy percentage of the Jaintia Hill was 35.32 which was lower than that of the Meghalaya state (49.10). The percentage of literates among the females was higher 36.31 per cent compared to that of males (34.3%). In the urban area, the literacy percentage was 81.37 and in the rural areas it was 30.35% . The percentage of total working population was 49.36 in 1991. The percentage of male workers (56%) was found to be higher than the female workers (43%) and the majority of the workers were found in rural areas (51%) than in urban areas (35%). This is because of the children and young men and women were the students in urban areas but in rural areas most of this section of population are participating in agriculture and household jobs.

The Jaintias live in 459 village and only 20,601 persons are found to live in the lone town Jowai, the headquarters of the district. In 1971 the population of Jowai was 8,927 and the same increased to 12,908 in 1981 which meaned Jowai town had shown an increase of 7693 persons over the decade 1971-1981. Jowai is linked with the rural areas of the district and acts as an important centre of trade, commerce, education, health, recreation etc. for the south eastern region of Meghalaya.

CONCLUSION

The geographical frame work including climate as discussed earlier has direct bearing on the distribution of population, settlements and linkage pattern of the district. In the past the Jaintias enjoyed the advantage of a well balanced ecology with available natural resources including foodstuffs. They had like other tribals a non exploitative socio-economic structure, freedom from indebtedness and other forms of dependence on non-tribals. But now their traditional style of life has been disrupted by disaster effect of modern civilization and materially by non-tribals who invaded their habitat. The subsistence tribal structure of the economy has now been broken down and the entire Jaintia Hills is now in a state of socio-economic transition warranting socio-economic development without disrupting the traditional setup of the region.

REFERENCES

1. Pascee, E.H. 1950, A Manual of the Geology of India and Burma, Vol. I, Govt. of India Press. P. 241.
2. Barch, H., 1986 The History and Culture of the Khasi People, 1986, Spectrum publications, Guwahati P.46
3. Gait E. 1984 A History of Assam, LB S Publications, P.259.
4. Chakravarty, M., 1995 "Differential Fertility and Infant Mortality among the Jaintias of Meghalaya : A study on Bio-Social Correlates", Unpublished Ph.D. Thesis, Gauhati University, P.34).

2

ECOLOGICAL VIEW OF JAINTIA HILLS – ITS ENVIRONMENT, LAND AND PEOPLE (A Critical Assessment)

B P Dey

LOCATION

Meghalaya – 'An adobe of clouds' is one of the seven states of the North East. Beautiful Jaintia Hills is a part of Meghalaya. It is situated between 25°3" to 25°45" North latitudes and 91°58" to 92°47" East longitudes. It is bounded on the North and East by the state of Assam. On the South by Bangladesh and on the West by Khasi Hills district. Its Headquarters town:

Fig..1

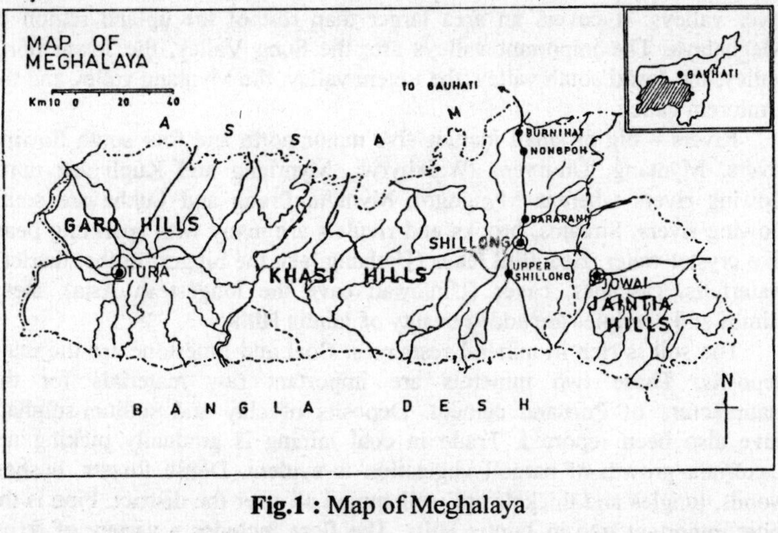

Fig.1 : Map of Meghalaya

Jowai is located at a distance of 64kms from the state capital along the Shillong-Silchar National highway – 44. A picturesque town circled by the majestic Myntdu river. It connects the capital with regular transport facility.

ENVIRONMENT

Shillong is located at an altitude of 1496 metres above sea level. Shillong capital of Meghalaya is often termed as "Scotland of the East". It is the most popular holiday destination in the North East. Jaintia Hills is an extension and integral part of Meghalaya. A hill resort similar to East Khasi Hills, unique in its scenic beauty and culture. Like any other environment, it is a combination of so many components such as light, temperature, soil, water etc. which surrounded and influence all organisms such as plants, animals and people of Jaintia Hills. Any external force, substance or condition which influence the life of an organism in any way, become the factor of its environment. Factors may be therefore, non-living (abiotic) or living (biotic) and the place where an organism lives – habitat indeed provides a particular set of conditions – the environmental complex.

The direct factors of East Khasi Hills such as intensity of sunlight, temperature (min 5°C to max 24°C), rainfall (7912 mm, 1995), relative humidity (min 55% and max 93%), wind, slopes, steepness and exposure of slopes, direction of mountain chains, valleys and different forms of life (plants, animals and micro-organisms etc.) are almost similar to Jaintia Hills though there may be some variations.

LAND

Jaintia Hills covers an area of 3819 sq kms. It is a remarkable hilly tract with a chain of hillocks. The upper region of Jaintia Hills has extensive river valleys. It covers an area larger than rest of the upland region of Meghalaya. The important valleys are: the Sung Valley, the Jowai north valley, the Jowai south valley, the Letein valley, the Myntang valley and the Umiurem valley.

Rivers – big or small include five major north and four south flowing rivers. Myntang, Umiurem, Waikhyrwi, Mynriang and Kupli are north flowing rivers whereas Myngngot, Myntdu, Prang and Lukha are south flowing rivers. Streams, brooks and rivulets are many with sparkling pearl like crystal water. Beautiful lakes (Umhang lake the biggest in the district), waterfalls, cascades, caves (Umlawan cave the longest in Asia), steep climbs and precipies are added beauty of Jaintia Hills.

The soil is rich in mineral resources. Coal and limestone are the main deposits. These two minerals are important raw materials for the manufacture of Portland cement. Deposits of clay and sodium-sulphate have also been reported. Trade in coal mining is gradually picking up. Luxuriant growth of natural vegetation is evident. Dense forests, bushes, woods, jungles and thickets are well spread all over the district. Pine is the most important tree in Jaintia Hills. The flora includes a variety of ferns, mushrooms and large number of orchids. Similarly, fauna include many birds and animals. The fascinating carnivorous plant called Pitcher Plant (Nepenthes Khasiana) are found at Jarain in Jaintia Hills.

PEOPLE

The vast majority of population include Scheduled tribe : 210558, Scheduled Caste: 747 and remaining others. The population density is 58 per sq km. The Jaintia people are industrious and enterprising. They evince keen interest in trade and commerce inspite of low literacy rate. The people inhabiting in the district are: Pnars, Wars, Bhoi (Karbis) and Biates mainly. The Jaintias do not have their script, the language spoken is Khasi. They have no vernacular of their own.

The Jaintia believe in egalitarian society where everybody is regarded as equal. In social relationship, there is no rigid caste or class system. A sense of unity within the society is praiseworthy. The Jaintias believe in a socially approved marriage. It resembles a Hindu joint family. The role of a maternal uncle as the manager of the family affairs in place of father is another unique feature. The Jaintias take interest in community activities. Hence they have many community buildings calleed 'Lung Walieh' used for community gathering, staging dramas, variety shows and plays often organised based on mythological to modern themes, located at Jowai.

Marriage among the Jaintia is an elaborate one though many changes are noticeable due to factors like Christianity, education and exposure to outside world. Like Khasi custom, the rule of inheritance of property is purely matrilineal. Women are entrusted to take care of property as the legal custodian, the family purse, valuable, movable and immovable properties.

ART AND CULTURE

The Jaintias are known for their rich art and culture. Hand woven traditional costumes worn during dances and festivals will draw anybody's attention and earn appreciation.

At Larnai village, earthen pots known as Kchu larnai are manufactured without the potter's wheel. Lac or red resin dye is also important like that of pottery industry of the Northern Jaintia Hills.

Cane, bamboo and wood are used for carving and engraving of various designs of craftwork. Pestles and mortars for pounding rice, handles for knives, daos, spate, hoes, canoes, baskets, trays, mats, sunshades, rainshades, containers and other articles are made by the Jaintias.

The Jaintia music and dance is very rich accompanied by different musical instruments such as bhuri (a clarionet like flute), bom (big drum), flute (ka chawiang) etc.

FESTIVAL

'Ben-dieng-Khlam' is a major festival celebrated in Jaintia Hills during rainy season normally in July or August every year. The festival through its rituals drive away the devil which causes destruction to crops, properties or miseries of people. The three days festival begins with sacrifices to 'U Mukhal' food offerings to departed souls of ancestors, chasing away the evils and dancing performance of the young and the old. On the last day in the morning the religious priest called Doloi accompanied by townfolk move from house to house beating the roof with sticks to drive away the plague. Later in the afternoon, well decorated 'rots' similar to those of tazias brought out during Muslim festival of Mohurram, one each from the seven localities of the town to the bank of a pool. Freshly cut poles of greate length from the forest are held across the stream. People jump on the poles and break them while dancing in the muddy water of the pool. Later a large pole is placed across the stream and the people dividing themselves into two parties contend for the possession of this pole in good humour.

The concluding part of the festival is 'Katlawakor' much like a game of football which is played between two parties, one representing the upper valley and the other the lower valley of the Myntdu river, with a wooden ball. The party which wins, believes would have better harvest than the other.

AGRICULTURE

Agriculture is the main occupation of Jaintia people. Wetland cultivation of paddy is the main crop grown by employing ploughs and bullocks. Source of water for irrigation is through well network of channels connected to hill streams and rivers as done in the plains. Other important crops such as bay leaves, pepper, oranges, betelnut, betel leaves are grown towards the south down slopes closer to the border of Bangladesh. Jaintia Hills produce turmeric well in demand outside the state and even in abroad.

ECOLOGICAL VIEW

In Meghalaya, population growth shows an increase from 16.69 lakhs in (1988-89) to 21.65 lakhs in (1997-98) – a steady growth trend in course of ten years with low density of population being 96 per sq km in Meghalaya as compared to all India increase of 298. Increase in total population of Scheduled Tribe from 80.64 to 89.18 per centage (1996) confirms the status of Meghalaya as a tribal state deserving a special treatment from rest of the country. Percentage of main workers include 52.2% whereas industrial workers are only 0.2%. Agricultural workers being 16.3% and non agricultural workers covers 31.5%.

Literacy percentage is 49.1% as aginst all India percentage of 52.2%. Urban population are more literate being 73.1% as compared to rural population of 44.7% only.

Cultivated area of Meghalaya is only 10.64 as compared to all India percentage of 57.24. This indicates Meghalaya is poor in agriculture but rich in its forest cover. The forest area is encouraging being 41.70 as compared to all India percentage of 19.27 only. Gross irrigated area (.000 hectare) and that of total percentage of cropped area of Meghalaya being 46 and 19.3 as compared to all India figures being 70640 and 37.5 respectively. Similarly, gross irrigated area per cultivator (hectares) and crop yield per hectare (kgs) of rice in Meghalaya is only 0.11 and 1346 as compared to all India figures being 0.59 and 1879 respectively (Table 1).

In view of prevailing situation, Jaintia Hills shares only 381100 hectares of utilised land which is 1/6 of the total area of 2240900 hectares of land in Meghalaya. Similarly, a little over 1/6 of the total area of the state is covered by forest in Jaintia Hills. The remaining include land not available for cultivation, uncultivated and fallow land mainly. Net area sown in 1/12 of the total area of Jaintia Hills as compared to 1/10 of total area of the state. The area sown more than once, covers only 240 hectares which is the lowest compared to all other districts of Meghalaya. The total area of Jaintia Hills is 33200 hectareas. (Table-2).

Number of small scale Industries in Jaintia Hills has 399 units with 1608 persons employed. The number of registered factory being only one with 28 employees. Total number of tourists spots in Meghalaya are: 62 of which Jaintia Hills has only 8 tourist spots (1997). (Table 3-5).

Table 1: Economic Indicators : Meghalaya and India

Sl. No	Items	1988-89		1993-94		1997-98	
		Meghalaya	All India	Meghalaya	All India	Meghalaya	All India
1	Population (in lakhs)	16.69	8193.21	19.33	9018.53	21.65	9811.17
2	Population growth rate (%)	(a) 24.92	(a) 19.58	(b) 15.82	(b) 10.05	© 12.00	© 8.81
3	Density per sq. km.	74	249	89	274	96	298
4	Effective Couple protection rate (all methods)	5.2 (1990)	43.3 (1990)	4.0	45.4	4.2 (1996)	46.5 (1996)
5	Scheduled Tribes as percentage of total population	80.64	8.05	87.07	8.15	89.18	8.38
6.	Scheduled Castes as percentage of total population	0.43	15.88	0.55	16.66	0.60	17.10
7.	Total main workers as percentage of total population	42.9	32.1	39.7	34.1	38.6	34.6
8.	Cultivators as percentage of main workers	57.7	40.2	54.5	37.9	52.2	36.9
9.	Agricultural Labourers as percentage of main workers	10.1	23.9	14.5	26.5	16.3	27.0
10.	Non-Agricultural workers as a percentage of main workers	32.2	35.9	31.0	35.6	31.5	38.1

Sl. No	Items	1988-89		1993-94		1997-98	
		Meghalaya	All India	Meghalaya	All India	Meghalaya	All India
11.	Percentage of industrial workers (manufacturing & household industries) to the main workers	0.7	3.4	0.3	3.7	0.2	3.8
12.	Literacy percentage (a) Total (b) Rural (c) Urban	 34.1* 27.5* 64.1*	 43.7* 36.1* 67.3*	 49.1** 41.1** 81.7**	 52.2** 44.7** 73.1**	 49.1** 41.1** 81.7**	 52.2** 44.7** 73.1**
13.	Cultivated area as percentage to total area	10.80	55.08	10.63	56.71	10.64 (1994-95)	57.24 (1994-95)
14.	Forest Area as percentage to total area	41.93	20.41	41.84	20.81	41.70 (1996-97)	19.27 (1994-95)
15.	Gross irrigated area ('000 hectareas)	49	59329	46	68367	46 (1994-95)	70640 (1994-95)
16.	Percentage of irrigated area to total cropped area	20.2	32.2	19.3	36.6	19.3 (1994-95)	37.5 (1994-95)
17.	Gross irrigated area Per Cultivator (hectares)	0.13	0.64	0.12	0.62	0.11 (1994-95)	0.59 (1994-95)
18.	Crop yield per hectare (kgs) (a) rice	963	1690	1128	1890	1346 (1996-97)	1879 (1996-97)

Note: * As per 1981 census
** As per 1991 census
(a) Growth in eight years
(b) Growth in five years
(c) Growth in four years
Q. Quick Estimates
N.A. information not available

PLENTY OF POTENTIAL FOR THE FUTURE

Jaintia Hills is unique in its physics, ecological, social and cultural diversity though it is now facing new challenges like in many other parts of India. Growing population is a great challenge with added pressure on its natural resources which reduces its development. True development means the development of human resources mainly. Once people are made literate through basic education, it will be possible to deal with the problem of population, poverty and environment which are interrelated. Ours is a rich land with poor people where about 40% of people are still below the poverty line in India. The vast majority of Jaintia Hills are directly dependent on the natural resources for their basic needs of food, fuel, shelter, and fodder. Environmental degradation has adversely affected the poor mainly, who depend upon the resources of their immediate surroundings. It is therefore necessary to deal with the problems of forest management, land and water at different levels on top priority basis. To arrest the loss of forest cover, an effort to regenerate forest by plantation of fast growing tree species such as Pine, Teak, Sal, Plywood etc. and intitiative by the Social forestry should be pursued vigorously. An effort towards sustaining a vibrant Hills ecosystem and preservation of Sacred Groves would be a wide decision rather than opting for short term immediate gain of development thorugh urbanisation. Intensive plantation will meet the multiple needs of fuel, fodder, fertilizers, food and medicine on the one hand and prevent degradation of natural forest land on the other. The natural habitat at both animals and wild life should be protected by creating biosphere reserves, national parks, wild life santuaries etc. No commercial exploitation should be allowed.

Table 2: District-wise Land Utilisation in Meghalaya, 1997-98

(Hectares)

Sl. No.	Items	East Khasi Hills	R1-Bhol	West Khasi Hills	Jaintia Hills	East Garo Hills	West Garo Hills	South Garo Hills	Meghalaya
	1	2	3	4	5	6	7	8	9
I	Reporting Area	275200	237800	530100	381100	260300	371400	185000	2240900
1.	Forest	104174	83914	205661	152155	122761	165740	100062	933998
2.	Not available for cultivation	48096	31628	72904	31265	10414	21997	9762	226066
3.	Other uncultivate land excluding fallow land	81650	86944	162277	138765	67647	62444	31839	631566
4.	Fallow land	10780	16073	68005	25955	30577	57830	24562	233782
5.	Net area sown	30969	19341	21252	32960	28901	63389	18775	215588
6.	Area sown more than once	7608	1506	4928	240	5224	19889	4717	44112
7.	Total cropped area	38577	20847	26181	33200	34125	83278	23492	259700

Source: Directorate of Economics & Statistics, Meghalaya.

Next to air, water is the important constituent of life support system. It is the most important natural resource and Jaintia Hills is blessed with water through its water bodies such as small rivers, streams, lakes, brooks, waterfalls etc. We depend on water for irrigation, domestic needs, sanitation and disposal waste mainly in our hilly region whereas big rivers, sea, oceans have been polluted by man due to industrial growth, urbanisation and other man – made problems in cities and towns. We need to explore these water resources for useful purposes including construction of mini and micro hydel projects, fisheries and agriculture etc with balanced utilisation of available water resources.

Table 3: Number of Small Scale Industries Registered with the Directorate of Industries

Year/District	Units (Nos)	Investment in Plant and Machinery (Rs. in Lakh)	No. of Persons Employed
1993-94	2094	1284.76	12042
1994-95	2294	1513.80	13483
1995-96	2533	1730.80	14791
1996-97	2765	1991.45	16104
1997-98	3008	2249.50	17259
1997-98 (District Wise)			
East Khasi Hills	1359	1327.26	9201
Ri-Bhoi	66	261.27	628
Jaintia Hills	399	254.58	1608
West Khasi Hills	560	167.80	2567
East Garo Hills	260	94.02	1299
West Garo Hills	317	133.60	1744
South Garo Hills	47	10.97	212

Source: Directorate of Industries, Meghalaya, Shillong.

We need to make judicious use of organic manure for soil fertility instead of synthetic fertilizers.

We should encourage traditional industires rather than manufacturing large-scale industries.

Dependence on fossil fuels such as coal, petrol and diesel should be reduced and tapping of solar energy should be expanded.

In Jaintia Hills alone, there are more than fifty places of interest. These places may be developed as tourist spots to attract tourists from outside. Tourism is now accepted and promoted as an Industry and gained a new impetus globally.

Once we learn to live with nature and how to conserve it, nature will take care of us and grant a normal healthy life to lead. We should therefore make an all out effort to explore plenty of potential as – resources for welfare of the people and Jaintia Hills of Meghalaya.

Table 4: Industry and Mining : Number of Registered Factories in Meghalaya

Year/District	Units	Employees
1	2	3
1990	58	3345
1991	55	2478
1992	55	2439
1993	53	2604
1994	56	2746
1995	58	2800
1996	58	2822
1997	65	2929
1997 (District wise)		
Jaintia Hills	1	28
East Khasi Hills	36	1621
Ri-Bhoi	20	922
West Khasi Hills	–	–
West Garo Hills	3	86
East Garo Hills	5	272
South Garo Hills	–	–

Source: Chief Inspector of Boilers & Factoreis, Meghalaya.

Table 5: Tourism – Number of Tourist Spots in Meghalaya

Sl. No.	District	1993	1994	1995	1996	1997
1	2	3	4	5	6	7
1	East Khasi Hills	20	21	21	25	26
2	West Khasi Hills	2	2	2	3	3
3	Ri-Bhoi	–	4	5	5	5
4	Jaintia Hills	5	5	5	6	8
5	East Garo Hills	2	3	5	4	4
6	West Garo Hills	2	8	8	9	9
7	South Garo Hills	3	7	10	8	7
	Meghalaya	34	50	56	60	62

Source: Directorate of Tourism, Meghalaya

REFERENCES

1. 1991 Census, Govt. of Meghalaya.
2. Directorate of Economics and Statistics, Meghalaya.
3. Directorate of Industries, Meghalaya, Shillong.
4. Chief Inspector of Boilers, Meghalaya.
5. Directorate of Tourism, Meghalaya.
6. Shillong Travel and Tele Guide, Meghalaya Tourism.
7. Meghalaya Yesterday and Today, PR Kyndiah.
8. Jaintia Hills District, Silver Jubilee Celebration, 1972-1997.

3

THE JAINTIA HILLS : LAND, PEOPLE AND ITS ENVIRONMENT

F Suchiang

BACKGROUND INFORMATION

The Jaintia Hills District is situated in the eastern most part of the State of Meghalaya. It is bounded by Karimganj and North Cachar District of Assam in the east, the Karbi Anglong District of Assam in the north, Bangladesh in the south and the East Khasi Hills District of Meghalaya in the West. If one is to develop a clean idea about the Jaintia Hills, he should flash his mind to the decades before 1947-48 when the area of the then Jaintia Hill Sub division was more than 4000 square kilometers. It included some areas, which were subsequently transferred to Karbi Anglong and the Jaintiapur Sub division of Sylhet District of Bangladesh. After the partition of the country, few of the pockets of Jaintia inhabited areas have been transferred to the erstwhile East Pakistan. Similarly, after the creation of the Karbi Anglong, an area of about 300 square kilometers have been slashed out of the then Jaintia Hill Sub division and annexed to the then newly created Mikir Hill District. After all the above factors the area left is only 3819 square kilometers. The altitude varies from 1500 meters in the hilltop down to 100 meters in the foothills bordering Bangladesh. It lies between the latitude 25.1° North and the longitudes 91.1° and 92.4°East.

On the basis of physiography, like topography, relief drainage, the district may be divided into 3 parallel zones. The Northern zone is composed of the gentle hilly slopes draining into Brahmaputra valley of Assam through Karbi Anglong and North Cachar Hill District. The natural vegetation is composed of about 60 percent broad leaf species and about 40 percent of conifer. The central cone is composed of the undulating plateau land where about 75 percent of the vegetation are made up of conifers-Pinus Kesiya and hardly 25 percent are broad leaf species. Most of the rivers that flow into Brahmaputra Valley and Surma Valley originate from this plateau. The southern zone is composed of steep slope draining into the Bark Valley of Assam and the Surma Valley of Bangladesh. The natural vegetation in the southern zone is composed of broad leaf species only. In fact, the southern zone is renowned for the cultivation of cash crop like pan, betel nut, tezpatta, piper oblongum and piper nigrum etc.

Presently, most of the areas in the district have been made accessible by the construction of network of roads linking the interior areas with the district headquarters and the other part of the state. The National High way 44 connecting the Barak Valley of Assam, Tripura, Mizoram and even some parts of Manipur with rest of the country virtually run through the heart of the district. Thus high way is one of the busiest high ways in the country.

The Jaintia Hills, as it is today, is inhabited mostly by the Jaintias or the Pnar, which are also at times, called the Syntengs. Besides, Jaintia Hills, sizeable numbers of the Pnars or the Jaintias are found all over Shillong. Few pockets of the Shillong City, like the Wahthapbru, the Sunny Hills, Quallapatti and even lower Mawprem are inhabited mostly by the Jaintias. In search of livelihood, many of them have migrated to different parts of North Eastern region like the Jatinga in North Cachar Hills and Karimganj District of Assam. Many of them have migrated even to the foothills of Nagaland, Mizoram, Tripura and Manipur. As of today, one may say that the Jaintias living in the other parts of the North Eastern region is equivalent to half of the population of the Jaintias now living in Jaintia Hills itself.

The Jaintia or Pnar, is recognised as one of the Scheduled tribes under the constitution of India. About 50 years ago, the main occupation of about 70 percent of the people was the agriculture, where as about 30 percent of them before independence achieved their prosperity through trade and Commerce with Bangladesh and Assam. The produce of the cash crop from Assam and Jaintia Hills like pan, betel nut etc. are taken down to Bangladesh and while returning back, they used to bring with them commodities like sugar, clothes etc. for sale in the district. After partition in 1947, trade and commerce with the erstwhile East Pakistan, (now Bangladesh) was completely terminated for sometime. Consequently, the people living in the border areas had to suffer and their economy was at very low ebb. of late, the trade and commerce have been resumed under bilateral agreement and free foreign exchange. Similarly, the erstwhile 70 percent were very conscious about keeping and maintaining of forest groves in their private land. Unfortunately, nowadays the erstwhile love for forest has gone down and the people have become business minded that they have felled most of the nature's private forest in the district for commercial purposes. Their indigenous and inborn habit of raising plantations was more of an aided regeneration. Earlier, about 40 percent of the population of the district sustained in dry farming and shifting cultivation only. Immediately before abandoning the particular plot and shifting to another, the cultivator or jhumias used to insert branches of Pinus Kesiya containing matured comes at regular interval of about 2 meters only. The seeds that come out from the cones germinate very well. Every year the owners used to do fire protection and removal of the week saplings. Subsequently, these areas form beautiful pine plantations. With the development process that takes place in the district the love for these types of activities also started going down with many of Jaintias. In the process whatever has been clear felled by them, do regenerate on its own, but the annual fire hazard used to destroy the saplings and the areas remain barren for many years and the ecology in these places started degrading from forest ecology to grass land ecology.

The district is very rich in mineral resources like coal and limestone. The reserve of coal in the district is about 60 million metric tones. Except the northern zone bordering Karbi Anglong District of Assam, the entire district is full of coal and limestones. Coal is not of a very good quality because the Sulphur content is comparatively high. Therefore, the boiler of any factory using this coal has to be specially fabricated to be corrosive resistant. Limestone of course is of very high quality. Most of the coal and limestone that have been extracted are sent outside the state for feeding the industries in the other part of the country and the neighbouring country of Bangladesh. But inspite of the existence of these minerals the state is industrially still very backward. So far, only one mineral based industry, that is, the Jaintia, Cement Plant with a capacity of only 50 tons per day, has been established in the district. Coal is excavated as such and sold to the other parts of the country. Every day, at least 1000 truck loads of coal used to move out of the district. The mining of coal is done by open cast and rat hole method only, which are considered as most primitive system. This system has disfigured the earth's surface all over the district. The spoil that comes out of the mining site has silted up all the permanent wet paddy fields in low lying areas. The toxic water that comes out of these mining sites has polluted all the rivers and streams which has also killed all the aquatic life therein. Even those, which are alive, have gone down to Bangladesh where this pollution has almost been neutrlised. The spoil has also rendered the soil infertile. In the abandoned coal depot, not even a blade of grass can grow.

The main staple food of the people of the area is rice. Prior to 1950, the district was self sufficient in food grains. Three rivers are originating from and flowing through the district viz. The Myntdu, the Umiurem, Ialip and Myntang. All these rivers have created vast areas of flat land in their bank, which are suitable and ideal for wet paddy cultivation.

SOIL

The soil in the northern most strip of the district and in the river valley is alluvial and semi alluvial in nature. This soil is very deep. The northern strip, below that is composed of deep loamy soil. The central plateau is made up of Red soil and support good coniferous forest. On the other hand, the slope in the Southern aspect is composed of shallow sandy loam.

ROCK

The Southern and eastern slopes of these hills is composed of sandstone, granite and limestone. The limestone is of very high grades. These limestones are utilised locally for production of quick lime and the quick lime is sold out to tea gardens and paper mills in the neighbouring state of Assam. In tea gardens the lower portion of the stem is white washed with limewater to prevent attack from insects. Similarly, the limewater is used for whitening the paper in the paper mill.

Sandstones are chiselled into square or rectangular and used in construction of course retaining walls. The granites are blasted by dynamite, hammered into pieces to be used in road consolidation. Granite chips are used in black topping of roads and other R.C.C. works. Huge quantities of these limestones are also sold out to the cement factories in Assam and used agents to upgrade the quality of cement as their limestones are of inferior quality.

ENVIRONMENT

In general, the Jaintias are always ecological and environment friendly. About 5 (five) decades ago, the Jaintias never allowed any land to be left barren. That was why only most of the best high forest under conifers are available in Jaintia Hills. But with the opening of network of roads, and the discovery of coal belts in the district, most of the forest in the coal belt areas have been destroyed to make way for the excavation of coal.

As has been mentioned above, mining of coal is done in the most primitive way, namely, open cast and rat hole mining. In the process, the surfaces have been disfigured completely. The rivers and streams have been polluted and all the aquatic life therein, have been completely destroyed and eliminated. The paddy fields in the river bottoms have been silted and made unfit for raising any agricultural crops. Indiscriminate felling of trees took place for commercial purpose. At the instant of Business from outside, people became impatient for quick money. Need of the people have been converted into greed.

The big trees, have been replaced by young and middle -aged forest plantation. The total volume of the standing trees has gone down tremendously. But, area-wise, the forest is on the increase.

With the discovery of coal belts, many of those people who used to subsist in shifting cultivation, abandoned this profession overnight and switched over to coal business activities like digging of coal, transport of the same into the vehicles etc. Therefore, one can easily conclude that enviromnentally, the entire Jaintia Hill is still better and safe.

The other environmental problems that the district is facing includes air, water and sound pollution. All these pollutants comes out from the faulty mining and burning of coal and the increase in the number of vehicles that pass through the National Highway, NH 44. Efforts have been made to contain water pollution through both engineering and biological processes.

But in case of air pollution, the people are helpless until and unless Government come forward to mitigate this problem.

The new hydro-electric project at LEISHKA has been sanctioned in Jaintia Hills. This will submerge an area of 56 hectares. Compensatory plantations will have to be done to compensate the submerged vegetation. The catchment area of about 350 square kilometers will have to be treated with all environment conservation measures.

In fine, if little precaution is taken up, the environment of Jaintia Hills has still bright future.

The author was the Chief Conservator of Forest, Meghalaya.

4

LAND SYSTEM IN JAINTIA HILLS DISTRICT

Gita Pyal

LAND SYSTEM – A HISTORICAL EVOLUTION

Meghalaya is one of the seven North-eastern States in India. It attained statehood on 2lst January 1972. Earlier, it was part of Assam. The tribal inhabitants of Meghalaya are broadly divided into two Major Tribes - The Khasis and the Garos. Subsequently, Meghalaya is divided: into seven districts - East Khasi Hills, Jaintia Hills, Ri - Bhoi, West Khasi Hills, East Garo Hills, West Garo Hills and South Garo Hills. All the tribal groups inhabit distinctly in the territories which fall into three distinct divisions, namely, the Garo Hills, the Khasi Hills and the Jaintia Hills. Consequently, the Land Systems among the tribes, in terms of the historical evolution developed in different ways in these three different areas.

Traditionally, the Land System, developed in the Jaintia Hills, at grass-root level is almost the same as that in the Khasi Hills. However, the Jaintias have got some written chronicles since the Ahom Period. It is related to historical records. Further, in about 1500 A.D., Parbat Roy, the ruling chief of the Jaintia hills extended his territory by conquest in the Southern plains and set up the capital of conquered area at Jaintiapur.

Prior to pre - British period, a three tier system of administration existed in the whole of Jaintia Hills. The syiem was at the top of the administration. Under him, at the zonal stage there were Dolois. At the lowest level of administration (village administration) there were village Headmen (Waheh Chnong). According to traditional set-up, the internal administration of the Land was carried out by the King (Syiem) with the assistance of 9 Dolois and 4 Sardars within their respective jurisdiction.

The British annexed Jaintia Hills in 1835. They declared the area as the British Area or Non-State. They abolished the office of the Syiem after the annexation. But the British sustained the two other offices of Doloi and village Headman to look after the administration of the area. The priest (the Langdoh) was deprived of his political power.

The Kingship (Syiem) was hereditary in character. Succession to the Syiemship was based on the matrilineal principle. That is the nephew (Sister's son) usually succeeded his uncle.

During the administration of the Rajas no revenue was paid by the people. The Raja controlled his subject in the plains directly. But in Hills Dolois was defacto sovereign. The Doloi rendered allegiance to the Raja by a nominal payment of small tribute of one he goat from each village and some parched rice for sacrifice during the pujas under his jurisdiction. The Raja's income was derived from duties on imported articles and rents from his own private land. The Raja's officials were allowed to appropriate a share of the produce from the land they held. They were not paid salary.

More so, the Syiem (Raja) was assisted by Raj Dorbar and a council of .Ministers (Myntries) the Langdoh (the Priest) Barkandazes, Choudhuries or the collectors of revenue and Zamindars, the owners of vast lands. The administration of the Hill areas was carried on with the consent of the dolois. In theory the Jaintia Raja was an absolute ruler of the Plains and titular ruler of the Hills. In the Hills areas, the dolois was the absolute ruler. They were the feudal despots. The Raja had nominal authority over the Dolpis. The Dolois controlled all the affairs of his Elaka (territory). The power of the Pators and Waheh Chnong were reduced. The Dolois became a Commission agent of the British. The doloi derived more powers and exercised more authority over his subjects as the British supported him at all times.

At the out set, the British government follow the same Jaintia System of accepting the he goat. But in 1858, Mr. Allen a high official of the Bengal Presidency visited the area. He proposed changes in the prevailing system. So the annual tribute of accepting a he goat was stopped altogether. It was also suggested to impose some sort of tax on land or household.

Subsequently the land was surveyed but no land revenue was imposed. Instead, a house tax of Re 1/- per house hold was introduced. People objected to pay such a house-tax. Openly they were up against the British as rebels and they were promptly put down. The second rebellion took place with the introduction of the central income tax. This was also suppressed 15 months later in 1863. The income tax exemption limit was raised. As a result an insignificant number of person in Jaintia Hills are to pay the income tax. So, the hostility against the payment of income tax was partly mitigated while the house tax was kept intact.

In 1869, the Jaintia Hills was formed into a sub-division with Jowai as its headquarters. It was a part of the united Khasi Jaintia Hills District in Assam. Steps were then taken to bring "the land under proper system of settlement. The whole Jaintia Hills was declared as `British Area' and was treated as the absolute property of British government. In the beginning, house-tax per house was assessed on Jaintia population and land was being exempted from taxation.

In 1882, Mr. Heath the then sub-divisional officer of Jaintia Hills carried on an enquiry and submitted a report in 1884. First of all, he had divided all land into two classes according to productivity and location.

These were
(i) Hali on low lands were terraced and permanently cultivated and irrigated with the help of either rain water or stream water.
(ii) High land which lacks irrigation.

The land tenure was classified by Mr. Heath as follows:
(i) Rajhali Land
(ii) Buniaz (Private) hali Land.

The high land was classified into:
(i) Government waste land.
(ii) Private high land

Mr. Heath then divided the 19 doloiship into 4 groups and the 4 Sardarship into another group according to location. Of these 5 groups the first three were located in the heart land, the fourth in the south slopes and fifth (Sardarship) in the northeast periphery. The northern slopes and the Southern slopes (i.e.) groups 4 and 5) had no hali land and also the third group (which had no haliland). The hali land was thus confined only to first and the second groups covering 10 Doloiships.

The British Government recognized no rights in the high lands but allowed them to be cultivated by anyone paying the house tax. The net result of the Government order of 1884 was both Hali land and High land were divided into two broad classes thereby making 4 distinct classes:
i) Private (Buniaz) hali land not assessable to land revenue.
ii) Rajhali land assessable to land revenue.
iii) Private high land not assessable to land revenue and
iv) Other high lands being the property of Government assessable to land revenue, if permanent cultivation was done.

Area of land in the Jaintia Hills known as Rajhali have been assessed for the purpose of land as Ryotwari since 1887. The irrigated or Low land, on the other hand, had the following types of ownership and control:

(i) **Raj Land :** Raj land belonging originally to Jaintia King or Raja, now the property of Government were assessed and subjected to land revenue are commonly known as Rajhali Land.
(ii) **Sanad Land or Sanna and Choudhury Land :** The Sanads and Choudhury were middleman who collected rents and paid them to the dolois or chiefs who inturn paid to the Raja or the King. And the Raja

on King paid them for their services by rent free grants of Sanna and Choudhury land.

(iii) **Service Land** : This category of land belonged to administration officers like Dolois, Pators and other officials who carried-out local administration. Sometimes these service land were assessed to revenue and paid by the doloiship through retained rent free by the doloiship and their officials.

(iv) **Village Puja Land** : There are some lands in the village kept separately and used entirely only for pujas purposes. These are revenue free and belonged to the doloi. The occupants paid the rent to the Doloi through the Laugdoh (the Priest) who rented the land from the Doloi for religious purposes only.

(v) **Private Land** : This land was held by individual as private property. The individual had the right to inheritance and transfer over this land also called Buniaz and could be transferred, mortgaged or sold. These land are also not assessed to revenue.

As regards High Land, these are sub-divided into:

(i) **Private Land** : This land had the same sort of tenure as the 'Hali' private land had.

(ii) **Unclaimed or Government Waste Lands** : This type of land could be cultivated by anyone on payment of rent.

The Government today has not assessed any revenue on private lands, though revenue on Rajhali land was assessed at the uniform rate and periodic leases were issued to the land holders.

After Independence, the Jaintia Hills formed a part of the united Khasi and Jaintia Hills Autonomous District under the sixth schedule of the constitution. The power of making laws for management and allotment of land in the district was vested to the District council under clause 3 of the schedule. The Dolois are controlled by the District council. The District Council has the power to regulate succession of appointment and removal of dolois.

According to the report on Agricultural census the Jaintia Hills District is divided into twenty circles called `elakas'. Eighteen of these circles are controlled by the Dolois, one by the Sardar, while one is under the direct control of the District Council. Land under each `elaka' is divided into 3 categories as mentioned earlier.

Revenues as stated earlier were imposed only on the Rajhali land but not on the Buniaz or non transferable land and service land. This system of land tenure is similar to the Zamindary System prevailing in the Jaintia Plains though in a small scale.

Thus, the traditional Pnar economy and society continue to exist till today and this is particularly true of the Niam tre Pnar or the Traditional

Pnar. The traditional Pnar social System was based on land. They were agriculturists having both permanent and shifting cultivation system. Therefore land is a source of the people's livelihood. It is centre of common interest and the people are very much sentimentally attached to it. The leading families of clan went to an area, claimed and occupied the lands, which they distributed among the members of their families. In course of time, through continued possession by cultivation, these families claimed absolute rights of ownership over such lands.

The land tenure system is the most problematic question amongst the Pnars because of their historical attachment with land. It should always belong to the people and not to the rulers or the Government. Though the Jaintia Raja had landed property in Rajbari area, from where he collected land taxes and rents.

In short, the land tenure system in Meghalaya varies from district to district. This is so because the system is based on tribal customs and traditions.

REFERENCES

1. Das, N.K., Ethnic Identity Ethnicity and social Stratification in North-East India, Inter-India Publication, New Delhi, 1989, p.155
2. Das, J.N., A study of the land system of Meghalaya, Law Research Institute Eastern Region, Guwahati High Court, Guwahati, Sponsored by North Eastern Council, Shillong, 1990, pp. 117-124.
3. Gurdon, P.R.T., The Khasis, London:Mac Millan, 1914, pp. 86 - 87.
4. Rao, V.V., B. Pakem and N.Hazarika: A century of Government and Polities in North East India, Vol II (Meghalaya) (1974 - 1983), Publishing by S. Chand and company Ltd, New Delhi, 1984, pp. 75 – 76.
5. Sinha, A.C., P.M., Chacko and I.E. Aier, Hill cities of Eastern Himalayas Ethnicity, Land and Relations and Urbanization, Indus Publishing House, I.E. New Delhi, 1993, pp. 114 - 115.

5

SOME RESOURCE BASED INDIGENOUS LAND USE SYSTEMS IN KHASI AND JAINTIA HILLS

K.K. Satapathy

INTRODUCTION

The central and the eastern parts of Meghalaya consisting of Khasi and Jaintia hills covers an area of 14375 km2. Physiographically it may be sub-divided into three sections, the northern hills, the central plateau and the southern hills. Based on rainfall, terrain and soil characteristics, the area can be broadly classified into three agro climatic regions, namely temperate zone, sub tropical hill zone and subtropical plain zone. There is a great variation of rainfall from north to south. This is primarily because of the higher altitude of the central zone in Khasi and Jaintia hills having almost east west direction which gives an rain shadow effect to the low lying northern areas. The acidic soil, undulating topography, soil erosion and degradation, ecological imbalance, abundance of weeds, insect pests and diseases and low level of technology are some of the biophysical constraints limiting agricultural production of the area. Farming systems based on scientific land use has not been studied adequately in the region. Cultivation of tuber crops such as potatoes, sweet potatoes and ginger on a series of beds formed along the slopes of the hills is widely practised in the area. Although good yield of crops have been obtained in the system, yet it leads to large amount of soil erosion which may be up to 40 to 50 tonnes of soil loss per ha. There are, however, a number of agricultural systems, practised in the area some of which are considered to be good farming systems. Farmers have created many farming patterns including multi layer agricultural, animal husbandry farming systems and home gardens in order to maximise production. In the hilly areas, several models of comprehensive management are practised. Planning forest trees on hill tops is a priority for controlling erosion and to improve ecological environment. In the middle slope fruit trees are grown. In the foot hills, where the slope is gentle, the soil is rich and water sources are plentiful, farm lands are developed by constructing ponds and check dams; aquatic production is developed in water bodies. Such comprehensive management integrates long term benefits with medium and short term ones. The possibilities of modifications to make improvements acceptable by the people need to be explored. Some of the traditional resource based management systems are mentioned below:

TRADITIONAL AGROFORESTRY SYSTEMS

Agroforestry is an age old practice in the North Eastern Region, where trees are : integrated extensively in the crop and livestock production systems depending upon agroclimatic and other local conditions. The characteristics of these agroforestry systems can be defined by a range of diverse products. Pine apple, areca nut, mandarin orange, citrus, betel vine, black pepper, jack fruit are the dominant species. Some fodder trees are in variably grown along with crops such vegetable, beans, cucurbits, ginger etc. characterized by a range of plant species with combination varying from house to house to meet a range of needs from food to shelter and the surplus sold in local market. A number of forest tree species are still being maintained or grown in shifting cultivation areas. The best examples are Pinus Kesaya and bamboos in Meghalaya and Alnus nepalenthasis in Nagaland. Bamboo resources are high value potential crop for agroforestry with short gestation and recurring return. The entire north eastern hill region is characterised by extensive bamboo formation which have considerable socio-economic value.

In Meghalaya Arecanut + betel vine/black pepper and broom grass+schemes/pinus Kesiya (khasi pine) systems are commonly practiced on the most degraded and bouldry lands with high slopes and shallow soil depth. All the systems/practices are well maintained in complete absence of chemical fertilizers under rainfed conditions. The productivity of the crops are basically resource based. All weed biomass and crop residues are completely recycled in situ which serve to conserve soil moisture and add substantial nutrient. Arecanut based mixed land use such as Arecanut + pine apple + betal vine/black pepper + mandarin orange is widely practiced in subtropical zone. Mandarin orange is also widely practiced and intensively intercropped with annual crops. This is possible because the erect habit of the plant provides very less shade for the intercrops. Singh et al (1994) in an investigation on traditional AFS, found that soil pH increased by 0.6 to 1.7 units within 10-15 years of practice in arecanut + black pepper + pine apple. In arecanut + cinnamon + black pepper + miscellaneous tree systems, at the same time exchangeable AI content - a potential cause of acid soils, completely disappeared due to addition of fresh organic matter.

A maximum accumulation of 2.91 % organic content was reported under arecanut + Jackfruit + black pepper + cinnamom followed by 1.85% in arecanut + betel vine + miscellaneous trees. The soluble contain such as

Ca, Mg & K were highest in arecanut + black pepper + jack fruit etc. (Dhyani et. al.'94).

BROOMGRASS - A HIGH VALUE CASH CROP

Broom grass (Thysanolaena maxima) - a grass with soil conservation value and established market as cash crop are grown in wastelands either by itself or as an undergrowth with sparsely distributed bay leaf (Cinnamomum obtusi folium). Broom grass is a shrubby plant which becomes 1.5 - 3.5 m tall, erect and normally forms a small thicket / clumps of about 2-4 ft diameter. This elegant grass is perennial in nature which bears the solid seed like culms. The barren hill slopes / hillocks, wastelands, discarded jhum fields can be utilised for cultivating these species. The grass protects soil from erosion and prevent the landslides and has wide scope for multiplication without any care or any protection. Hill slopes and the undulated hillocks are also suitable for them, which ascends up to an altitude of 2000 m. Used for making brooms, the grass is planted during May-June, after the plot is burnt. Harvesting is done at yearly intervals for a period of about 7 years. Subsequently, the grass is burnt and replanted. Weeding is done once or twice a year. Broom grass yield increased with plantation age up to 3 years and stabilized during the subsequent 3-7 years. When the roots settled in the soil it flourishes vigorously and gradually forms a clump by producing a large number of seed like culms. The grass is available in large quantities during months of June to December and is used as cattle feed both in summer and in the period of scarcity during winter. Broom grass remains green during dry winter months and produces spike for broom (a cash earner), leaves for fodder and stem for fuel or pulp material for coarse quality paper. Trials have shown that it is in no way inferior to many other cultivated fodders due to its nutritive value . The fine root systems of broom grass are well ramified up to 30-40 cm soil depth and has enormous soil conservation value on hill slopes. It can be used as terrace bund/riser stabilization also as vegetative contour hedge barrier for terraced land development.

WET RICE AND TERRACE CULTIVATION

Valley agriculture is practised throughout the hilly terrain both al low and high elevations. It is a sedentary form of wet rice cultivation and is a complementary system to jhum. It is done wherever terrain permits on flat lands between hill slopes; the soil in valley lands is fertile due to nutrient washout from the hill slopes. Bullock power is used for ploughing. The land utilization for double or multiple cropping is rather poor and monocropping is practised in general. However, there are areas where double cropping is practised. Bench terraces are well adapted in some areas more particularly in mild slopes with irrigation facilities. The bench terrace cultivation with availability of irrigation water represent an excellent example of using steep slopes and even rocky lands where small quality of soil is available for developing bench terraces and maintaining desirable production. However, there is dearth of sufficient plain land suitable for permanent cultivation. What ever plain land available is far less than the requirement of people for wholesome subsistence. The average size of land under valley cultivation for a family of five members consisting of two adults and three children is .5 to 1 ha larger families may have land area up to 2 ha (Ramakrishnan'93, Borthakur'92)

DRIP IRRIGATION USING BAMBOO

This system is practised by the farmers in Jaintia Hills to irrigate arecanut and betelvine grown on steep slopes with bouldry soils. Bamboo drip irrigation is a unique example of efficient management of available water and reflects the foresightedness of the tribal farmers. This system of water management is based on the principle of gravity flow which has been exploited by the tribal farmers. In this system small hill streams from upper reaches are diverted into bamboo fitted about 1 to 2 m above the ground surface with the support of bamboo stands. The water diverted from source is taken to lower reaches of the hills and elevation differences between the water source and site of its use may be as high as a few hundred meters. The rate of water flow varies from 800 to 1200 litres per hour. The water, brought to the field by these channels gravitationally and distributed through secondary, tertiary or more branches of pipe line with a typical water diversion system at the individual plants enabling the system to deliver 15 to 25 litres water per minute at the terminal of these branches. The water is allowed to trickle down drop by drop at the plant site by having small holes at appropriate point in the bamboo channels. The bamboos of various diameters (50-100 mm or more) are required to adjust the rate of flow of water. Bamboos of large diameter are used at the start from carrying maximum quantity of water in the beginning and the size can subsequently be reduced as per requirement of water. In bamboo drip irrigation system, water distribution from one channel to another is the key of success for running of the system properly. This is done with great skill at every stage to achieve the goal of water application judiciously and economically at the plant positions in the form of dripping in drops. Because the tribal people have a good habit of working in cooperation and harmony, it helps in successfully running of the system like many other community works (Singh' 89, Prasad et.al. '94).

CURING OF ARECA NUT

People of Meghalaya are fond of taking fresh Arecanut instead of processed one. But fresh fruits are not available round the year as the harvesting periods in the areas are November to December and March to April. Some of the produce is disposed off in the market, whereas slightly immature fruits are cured to improve their quality. The Khasis cure the areca nut in the flowing water. The water used to be changed every week. A pond for the curing of areca nut is constructed of stones and masonry. It is normally in the size of 15 m length, 10 m width and 2.5 m depth. Such a pond can take 150 baskets of nuts. The perennial stream is the main requisite for the location of a pond. In the typical arrangement, water flow is diverted from the up stream of the nearby pond at one end and outlet is kept diagonally opposite of the inlet. The water level maintained 2.35 m from the bottom with the continuous flow. The holding baskets are locally prepared of bamboo by matting of the size of 1 m diameter at top and 2.65 m height with the square bottom of 0.65m. The matting is done with 1 cm bamboo strips by keeping the 3cm perforation. Each basket has a capacity to hold 1200 kg of areca nut which is equivalent of 12 gunny bags of areca nut. A small bamboo basket is used for raising the cured fruit from the pond. This basket is matted in the size of 36 cm diameter a top, 30 cm high with the square base of 16 cm.

The pond is at first fragmented into the squares of 90 cm x90 cm each at the top with frames made of the strong bamboo. Thus the holding basket of 1 m diameter when inserted into these squares could be reduced to that size. The bamboo frames hold the individual baskets and keep them vertical. These baskets are filled with the freshly harvested areca nut. Fruits normally float on the water. The baskets are therefore covered with jute clothes and stone weights are kept over them in order to ensure the proper curing. Once the areca nuts are charged into the holding baskets, then they are not disturbed till the curing is completed. No special care is required except the maintenance of the water level of the pond and the water flow. The minimum water flow is assured (36 lt /min) to prevent the fruits from being spoiled. Excess water flow is considered good for keeping the fruit fresh. The criteria for adequate curing are : (i) Yellow colour turns prominently bright yellow and (ii) the husk gets freed from kernels. The normal curing time is around 4 to 5 months. The fruits are then taken out from the pond. The fruits are sometimes cured for one and half months and disposed as and when demand for them arises. Once the fruits are raised from one holding basket then that basket should be completely raised out otherwise the rest of the fruits will be spoiled. The loss in curing is generally 15-30% of the total weight. The loss can be minimised by keeping the same lot in one basket. The units of fresh fruits and nuts in one kilogramme amount to 42 and 75 in number respectively. The dry nuts in one kilogramme however amount to 135 in number. Curing improves colour, taste and freshness of ahe nut. Cured kernels are less astringent and are better to chew and taste (Jain et. al. '95).

REFERENCES

1. Borthakur D.N. (1992). Agriculture of the North Eastern Region. With special reference to hill agriculture. Beecee Prakashan, Guwahati.

2. Dhyani S.K Chauhan D.S. (1994); Agroforestry practices of North Eastern Hill Region of India Central Soil and Water conservation Research and Training Institute, Dehradun.
3. Jain, D. Satapathy, K . K.and Wahlang, E.L. (1995). Traditional Post Harvest Technology of North Eastern Hill Region, ICAR Research Complex for NEH Region, Barapani.
4. Prasad, R .N. & Sharma, V. C (1994). Potential Indigenous Farming Systems of North Eastern Hill Region, Barapani.
5. Ramakrishnan P.S. (1993). Shifting Agriculture and Sustainable Development. . Oxford University
6. Singh A. (1989). Bamboo Drip Irrigation System, ICAR Research Complex for NEH Region, Shillong.
7. Singh B.L., Dhyani S. K. and Prasad R. N. (1994). Traditional Agroforestry Systems and their soil productivity on degraded Alfisols/ultisols in hilly terrain. Interconference on sustainable development of degraded lands through Agroforestry, New Delhi Nov. 25 -30, 1994.

6

LAND UTILISATION AND PATTERNS OF ECONOMY IN JAINTIA HILLS : A Study of Recent Trends

Sutapa Datta and Susmita Das

Land is one of the most important resources of any region, which, inspite of being one of the most important components of the life support system, has been either under used or over used and even been abused by man. The trend is becoming more alarming in the recent decades in the country in general and in its hilly areas in particular. The hill areas of north eastern India were perceived even a couple of decades back as areas of dense forest and plenty of land. But the idea is steadily becoming a myth. Moreover, the region offers an ample base of resources for industries, and are being exploited since there is a general absence of large scale manufacturing industrial units. All these create a complex situation in terms of land use and resultant economy in the region.

The use or utilization of land primarily forms the basis of economy in any given area of the earth. Such a use can be any kind of permanent or cyclic intervention of man with the environment to satisfy his needs of food, clothing, shelter, etc., and such interventions are directly related to landuse. The different types of uses of land in any region are considerably influenced by its population number and its composition. This is particularly realized in areas of large concentration of rural population, since the economy of such a population is essentially land based.

The district of Jaintia Hills in Meghalaya is one such area where one can experience together the problems of ever increasing population; an overwhelming concentration of population in rural areas and limited cultivable land to feed the population. About two-thirds of the total population of the district being dependent on agricultural activities, makes it clear that utilization of the land in the district will have direct bearing on the economy of the people in this region. It is in this backdrop the present paper seeks to analyse the land utilization pattern in the Jaintia Hills district of Meghalaya and it's bearing on the patterns and characteristics of economy of the people in the area.

The main objectives of this study are:

(i) To analyse the land utilization pattern of the district at two points of time i.e., at 1980-81 and 1990-91;
(ii) To analyse the change in the pattern of land utilisation during this period; and
(iii) To analyse the impact of such changes on the economic conditions of people and on the environment as well.

DATA BASE:

The study is essentially based on secondary data obtained from:

a) Census Records
b) Various State Government Reports
c) Relevant Books, Periodicals and Journals, etc.

The work has been conducted mainly on district level, but as and when possible, the limit has been extended to community Development Block Level.

The collected data from various sources have been compiled in tabular forms and simple statistical techniques as percentages, ratios, etc. have been used to interpret the data.

ORGANISATION:

The present work has been organised in five broad sections. The first section deals with the general introduction and scope of the work as well as the introduction of the study area. This is followed by the second section, which analyses the land utilization scenario of the two periods 1980-81 and 1990-91 and the pattern of change over the period.

The third section deals with the economic composition of population in Jaintia Hills during 1991 and the pattern of change in the same from 1981 to 1991.

The fourth section is an attempt to analyse the impact of land utilization on the economy of the people of Jaintia Hills.

The fifth and final section summarizes the findings of the study.

THE STUDY AREA:

The district of Jaintia Hills is the eastern most district of Meghalaya, which encompasses an area of 3818 sq. km, i.e., about 17 percent of the state's total area. The district has three usual physical divisions like other areas of the state, namely, the central upland zone (Ri-Jaintia Country), the northern denuded hills (Pnar-Bhoi Country), the southern slopes (Pnar-War Country). The climate enjoyed by the district is monsoon subtropical. There are four Community Development Blocks (C. D. Blocks henceforth) in the districts, namely, Thadlaskein, Laskein, Khliehriat and Amlarem. As per 1991 Census, total population here is 220473 persons, of whom about 91 percent (199872 persons) is rural, and, thus, depend on land-based economies. The district does not have any major manufacturing industries.

II

Pattern of Land Utilisation:

The total geographical area of Jaintia Hills district has been classified into usual land use categories as (i) forest, (ii) land put to non-agricultural uses, (iii) Barren and uncultivable land, (iv) permanent pastures and other grazing lands; (v) land under miscellaneous tree crops and groves; (vi) cultivable waste land, (vii) old fallow, (viii) current fallow, (ix) net area sown and (x) area sown more than once. The distribution of land in these categories, however, is not uniform.

It appears form Table-I that, considerable area of the district is under forest, which is 39.93% in 1990-91. There has been a slight change in the coverage of forest from 1980-81, which was 37.91%. Though the amount of increase in forest land is small, it is quite significant for the district, as on the other hand there has been a decrease in the same in the state from 1980-81 onwards.

Table 6 : Percentage of land

	Land utilization	Percentage of land		
		1980 - 81	1990 - 91	1998 - 99
1.	Reporting Area*	100.00	100.00	100.00
2.	Forest	37.91	39.93	39.90
3.	Area not available for cultivation			
	a) Area under non-agricultural use	4.81	4.20	4.22
	b) Barren and uncultivable land	3.94	4.03	3.93
4.	Other uncultivated land excluding fallow land			
	a) Permanent pasture and other grazing land	-	-	-
	b) Land under misc. tree crops and groves	6.42	4.61	4.65
	c) Cultivable waste land	31.63	31.81	31.60
5.	Fallow land			
	a) Fallow other than current fallow	5.30	4.50	4.53
	b) Current fallow	2.17	2.30	2.43
6.	Net area sown	8.45	8.62	8.67
7.	Area sown more than once	0.03	0.05	0.08
8.	Total cropped area	8.49	8.68	8.75

Source: Land Utilization Statistics, Directorate of Economics and Statistics, Government of Meghalaya.

* Reporting area excludes the area under Municipality and Town Committee.

The district also has a considerably large share of land, which is uncultivable. In this category, however, there has been a decrease of land from 38.05% in 1980-81 to 36.42% in 1990-91.

Jaintia Hills has a very small proportion of its total area under cultivation, which is only 8.68% in 1990-91. From this only 0.05% is intensely cultivated being sown more than once. However, there has been a marginal increase of land under cultivation in the district from 1980-81 onwards (Table-1): As against this, quite a large proportion of land in the district is under non-agricultural uses, i.e., areas being not available for cultivation and fallow land. While the former takes about 8.23% of land of the district, the later takes about 6.80%. It may be mentioned here that the district has experienced a decline in the amount of land in both these above menrioned categories of land utilization over the period of 1980-81 to 1990-91.

The recent trend of utilization of land in the district (1998-99), however, indicates somewhat positive trend in certain categories, namely in current fallow and in total cropped area (Table-1).

III

The economic composition and occupation structure of the people in any area where rural land based economies are pre-dominated, are more or less inter related with the existing land utilization pattern. This is quite evident in Jaintia Hills.

WORK PARTICIPATION RATE:

Jaintia Hills district has a considerably large percentage of workers, which is 46.44% of its total population (Table-7). It is in this respect that the district shares a similar pattern not only with the state in particular but also with the other hill states of the region in general.

Table 7 : Work Participation Rate

Districts / C. D.Block	Area	Main Workers 1991	Main Workers 1981	Marginal Workers 1991	Marginal Workers 1981	Non-Workers 1991	Non-Workers 1981
Jaintia Hills	T	45.29	48.80	1.15	0.56	53.56	50.64
	R	46.53	50.00	1.13	0.61	52.34	49.39
	U	33.24	35.46	1.38	0.03	65.38	64.51
Thadlaskiem	T	44.20	39.91	0.83	0:60	54.97	59.48
	R	48.11	51.33	0.63	0.46	51.26	48.20
	U	33.24	35.46	1.38	0.03	65.38	64.51
Laskeim	T	43.17	46.26	1.14	0.81	55.69	52.93
	R	43.17	46.26	1.14	0.81	55.69	52.93
	U	–	–	–	–	–	–

Districts / C. D.Block	Area	Main Workers 1991	1981	Marginal Workers 1991	1981	Non-Workers 1991	1981
Khliehriat	T	49.23	54.62	0.82	0.09:	49.95	45.29
	R	49.23	54.62	0.82	0.09	49.95	45.29
	U	--	--	--	--	--	--
Amlarem	T	42.86	46.95	2.74	1.43	54.39	51.62
	R	42.86	46.95	2.74	1.43	54.39	51.62
	U	--	--	--	--	--	--

Source: Census of India 1981 & 1991, Series 14 & 16, Meghalaya, General Economic Tables.

A look into the spatial pattern of the distribution of working population (Table-2) in the district reveals that almost all the C.D. Blocks have a more or less uniformly high rate, with Khliehriat, however, having the maximum share of workers (more than 50%), while Laskein has the minimum (about 44% of its total population).

The area wise distribution of workers (Table-2) shows as a rule, a much higher percentage of rural workers than the urban once in the district and its constituent C. D. Blocks as well. The entire share of urban workers in the district is concentrated in Thadlaskein C. D. Block, which contains the only urban centre of the district.

The work participation rate shows a more or less uniform trend of change all throughout the district. It is to be noted here that though there has been a decline in the proportion of main workers, the share of marginal workers have shown a rise in all the spatial units of the district. This is quite spectacular in the case of the urban areas of the district.

Occupation Structure:

The majority of workers in the district as elsewhere in the State is engaged in primary sector of economy, more particularly in the farming activities and thus being directly dependent on land. Out of the total working population, about three-fourth (Table-3) is engaged in agricultural activities, either being cultivators (about 59%) or agricultural labourer (about 16%). The percentage share of workers in the secondary sector (about 0.2%) is negligible which in indicative of a very low level of industrial development in the district in particular. The share of workers in tertiary sector as a whole is quite significant being about 25% of its total working population. The majority of workers in this category are again engaged in service sector (being both clerical and professional) and in trade and commerce (about 1 1% and 6% respectively).

Table 8 : Occupation structure in Jaintia Hills

Districts / C. D. Block	Area	Cultivators		Agricultural lab.		Household Industry, . . . *		Other Workers . . . **	
		M	F	M	F	M	F	M	F
Thadlaskiem	91	56.97	60.05	11.20	15.90	0.19	0.17	31.64	23.88
	81	56.76	59.65	11.00	16.49	0.11	0.85	31.13	23.01
Laskeim	91	70.79	63.02	13.63	23.54	0.23	0.25	15.34	13.20
	81	82.58	80.59	6.45	14.12	0.28	0.46	10.69	4.84
Khliehriat	91	65.70	76.81	11.01	13.05	0.07	0.27	23.22	9.87
	81	69.55	84.64	7.81	9.73	0.04	0.20	22.59	5.44
Amlarem	91	20.85	21.20	21.72	29.44	0.15	0.64	57.28	48.73
	81	27.54	29.78	15.17	22.10	1.24	2.17	56.10	45.95
JAINTIA	91	57.63	61.41	13.06	18.16	0.15	0.27	29.16	20.16
HILLS	81	64.15	29.78	9.28	14.47	0.56	0.71	26.01	15.50

* Household Industry, Manufacturing Processing and Repairs (5a)
** All other categories 3, 4, 5b, 6, 7, 8, 9.
Source: Census of India 1981 & 1991, Series 14 & 16, Meghalaya, General Economic Tables.

A look into the areal pattern of occupation composition reflects a more or less uniform trend all throughout the district (Table-3). Almost all the C. D. Blocks of the district have a high share of workers in the primary sector than in the other two sectors. The only exception in this respect is Amlarem C. D. Block, which registers a much higher share of workers (about 53%) in tertiary sector than in the primary sector (37%).

Occupation structure in Jaintia Hills has quite significantly changed over the 'decade 1981-1991 (Tables-3 and 4). While the proportion of workers has declined in the primary sectors of cultivation and agricultural labourer as well as in livestock, fishing, plantation, etc., there has been a perceptible increase in the tertiary sector of economy. This is a trend, which is observed to affect mostly the rural areas of the district, which is further justified from the decrease of share of cultivators on the one hand and increase in the share of agricultural labourers on the other. It is only in Thadlaskein C. D. Block that an opposite trend can be observed (Table-3).

Table 9 : Industrial Category

Industrial Category	1991		1981	
	Male	Female	Male	Female
Cultivators	57.63	61.41	64.15	69.32
Agricultural labourers.	13.06	18.16	9.28	14.47
Livestock,...	3.86	2.66	7.63	4.83
Mining & Quarrying.	1.45	0.35	3.32	0.69
Manu. in HH. Ind.	0.15	0.27	0.56	0.71

Industrial Category	1991		1981	
	Male	Female	Male	Female
Manu. in other than HH Ind.	1.64	0.44	1.59	0.78
Construction	1.69	1.04	1.86	0.47
Trade & Commerce.	5.89	6.00	1.61	2.18
Transport	2.15	0.12	0.80	0.03
Other Services	12.46	9.54	9.20	6.51

Source: Census of India 1981 & 1991, Series 14 & 16, Meghalaya, General Economic Tables.

It is observed that, in the secondary sector of economy a marginal increase in the share of workers has taken place from 1981 to 1991, and this is again evident in Thadlaskein C. D. Block. The tertiary sector of economy, however, experiences an increase in the share of workers all along the district.

A look into the occupation structure of male and female population of Jaintia Hills shows that the share of female workers is higher in both primary and secondary sectors all throughout the district. However, the male workers outnumber the female workers in the tertiary sector. It may also be mentioned here that the share of male and female workers has maintained the same trend in both the census decades of 1981 and 1991 (Table-4).

IV

LAND, MAN, ECONOMY: AN INTEGRATED SCENARIO:

The economy of people being primarily land based in Jaintia Hills district of Meghalaya, it maintains a direct relation with the land utilization pattern. The distribution of land is not uniform under different categories of uses and this is further aggravated by expansion of villages, construction of roads, etc. As a result the cropland in the district is put to stress. As is evident from the changing pattern of land utilization in Jaintia Hills (Table-1) that it has not been possible to bring a perceptible increase in total cropland. Though there has been a marginal increase in the total cropland, this, in the context of a rapid increase in population appears to be quite insignificant. This not so significant increase in cropland is attributed to the factors like loss of top soil due to expansion of built up areas, improper farming practices like shifting cultivation, etc. The stress on the cropland is further understood from a gradual decline in per capita land holding. Basing on available data it is observed that per capita landholding has decreased from 0.54 hectare in 1980-81 to 0.44 hectare in 1990-91 in the district. It is also evident that the cultivable wasteland in the district does not show any significant change over the decade. All these may indicate that there is little scope for physical expansion of cultivable land in the district. Moreover, a continuous rise in area sown more than once from 1980-81 onwards indicates the pressure of increasing rural population on land which has forced the farmers to cultivate their land which more intensively in vertical dimension in the absence of adequate scope for the horizontal expansion of land.

The land-economy relation in Jaintia Hills is further understood from the landman ratios, which present a critical situation over the decade 1981-1991. It is evident from Table-5 that the agricultural* and physiological** densities, besides being much higher than the general density, also record a significant rise over the decade. This indicates a very strained relation between land and economy in the area. Though the densities could not be calculated for the C. D. Blocks of the district, the significant rise in their rural densities (besides general densities) land more or less similar interpretation.

Table 10 : High growth rate of population

District / C. D. Block	Growth Rate of Population 1981-91 (in %)	General Density 1981	General Density 1991	Rural Density 1981	Rural Density 1991	Agricultural Density 1981	Agricultural Density 1991	Physiological Density 1981	Physiological Density 1991
Jaintia Hills	40.96	41	58	38	52	184	226	486	672
Thadlaskein	75.34	70	104	50	78	NA	NA	NA	NA
Laskein	0.07	65	85	65	85	NA	NA	NA	NA
Khliehriat	51.43	21	31	21	31	NA	NA	NA	NA
Amlarem	37.68	55	75	55	75	NA	NA	NA	NA

Source: Census of India 1981 & 1991, Series 14 & 16, Meghalaya, General Economic Tables.

Another dimension of understanding the strained man-land ratio in Jaintia Hills is obtained taking note of changing proportion of cultivators and agricultural labourers. The rising number of agricultural labourer (Table-3) along with a high growth rate of population (Table-5) and a marginal risk in total cropped land in the district (Table-1) together explain an approach of a near stagnation in the primary sector of economy. This is further realized from a gradual decline of participation in primary sector of economy and consequent rise of the same in the tertiary sector particularly in the rural areas of the district. In the absence of any manufacturing industries in the district, there is hardly any scope of expansion of the tertiary sector particularly in trade, commerce and transport related activities. Such a pressure exerted by overwhelming land-based economy and the non-land based economy on each other demands an urgent need for further research.

$$* \text{ Agricultural density} = \frac{\text{Total Agricultural Population}}{\text{Net sown Area}}$$

$$** \text{ Physiological Density} = \frac{\text{Total Population}}{\text{Net sown Area}}$$

V

THE ANALYSIS CARRIED ON IN THE PREVIOUS SECTIONS CAN BE SUMMERISED AS FOLLOWS:

The general land use pattern in the district has usual ten standard categories. However, all the categories of land use pattern are not equally distributed all throughout the district. This variation is due both to physical and socio-economic factors.

The district experiences a marginal increase in total cropland, which is quite insignificant, compared to the total population growth. This along with an increase in area sown more than once reveals the limitations for physical horizontal expansion of land under cultivation on the one hand and intensification of cultivation of land in vertical dimension.

The agricultural labourer being constantly increased in the district along with a fall in cultivators affects the land-man ratio, which in turn tends to upset the sociocultural system of people in the district, since such a ratio challenges the, concept of egalitarian society, which is supposed to exist in the district and in the state.

It is evident from the occupation structure of population that the rural sector is not diversified since very small proportion of population is engaged in economies as livestock, fishing, plantation, etc. and in mining and quarrying. Moreover, a sharp fall in these activities brings about serious implication on land and economy of the people particularly in the rural areas.

The above findings indicate that the need of the hour is a thorough review of the existing land utilization patterns and its potentialities. It is also necessary to assess the inherent defects or loopholes of the existing land utilization system and find out the means to remove or minimize such defects.

A very positive feature that appears from the discussion that the area under forest in the district is on the rise. Though the amount of increase is marginal, it should not be overlooked considering the general situation in this aspect in the state and in the region. Thus, appropriate measures may be taken to explore the bearing of such increase in forestland on the economies of the district.

REFERENCES

1. Das, H. and Das, M. M. (1989): Land-use Pattern in the Pagladia-Puthimari Basin, Assam, in North-Eastern Geographer, Vol.21. No. 1 & 2, Guwahati.
2. Konwar, M. (1990): Land-use and Cropping Pattern in West Khasi District of Meghalaya, in R. K. Rai et. al. (eds.): Hill Area Development, The Geographical of North-Eastern Hill Region (India), Shillong.
3. Sharma, H. N. (1990): Integrated Land-use Planning: An Urgent Need of North-East India, North-Eastern Geographer, Vol. 22, Guwahati.

7

PEOPLE OF JAINTIA HILLS

Gita Pyal

At one corner of North-East India lies small state of Meghalaya. Primarily the state is composed of three ranges of hills - The Garo hills, the Khasi hills and the Jaintia hills, named after these hilly areas. The eastern part of Meghalaya is, specifically, known as Jaintia Hills. More specifically the District of Jaintia Hills is inhabited by a large number of tribal population known as Syntengs who dwell on the upland of central Khasi Hills. People of the deep valley and hillsides in the Southern part of the Jaintia Hills and East Khasi hills are called Wars. They have their own dialect. The Synteng known as Jaintias or Pnars, a sub-tribe of Khasi, is a scheduled Tribe. The Pnar of Jaintia are of Mongoloid race, speaking Austric Language belonging to the Mon-Khmer group who are migrated from East Asia.

The Jaintia who entered the Hills established themselves in different parts of the hills in social groups which came to acquire different names such as Amwis, Changpungs, Jowais, Nartiang. Raliangs and Sutngas. Each of the groups was under the governance of a priest (U Langdoh), the Mediator between people and their God. All the Jaintias were brought under one banner - during the Sutnga dynasty. Later on, a portion of the Syllhet plain was annexed to the Sutnga. All for that the state came to be known as Sutnga or Synteng and later on as Jaintia.

The Khasis and the Jaintias are different in certain traits of their culture due to ecological and historical reasons. They actually belong to a single tribe Austric speaking Indo- mongoloid. For this reason they are often called by a single appellation -the Khasis. They practiced a rigid form of Matrilinealism, one of the most ancient institutions of mankind.

People living in the Southern parts of both the Khasi and Jaintia Hills districts as well as in the border areas of Bangladesh are known as Wars but they could be differentiated from the Pnars or Synteng by their dialect. In the War area of Jaintia Hills, people of different villages speak different dialects which are totally different from the language spoken by the Khasis, Jaintia or Pnar. Unlike the different dialects spoken by different tribes of Nagaland, the War Jaintia have no problems in understanding each other's dialect. A person from one village may speak his/her own dialect to another person from a different village but they will fully understand each other. The difference is therefore not that wide except in pronunciation and in naming things. A Khasi or a Jaintia (non-war) would not understand any of the dialect except those persons who come into daily contact with War people themselves and that too, with great difficulty.

The area occupied by the War Jaintia, administratively fall under the jurisdiction of Doloiship of Jowai, Amwi, Satpator, Darang, and Nongtalang who otherwise have no clear-cut territorial demarcation of boundary lines. Thus, some villages situated right at the international border with Bangladesh are found to be under the jurisdiction of the Doloi of Jowai whose headquarters is at Jowai itself which is far away from the border area. Here people are, though, far away, live within his territorial jurisdiction but they still owe their allegiance to the Doloi and his administration. This system of political administration came about with the coming of the British who abolished the institutions of Kingship and of Priesthood - a three-tier system of administration that had been prevalent since the conquest of the Jaintia Hills in the 13th century A.D. The central authority then for the first time, had its own territory where its writs covered every aspect of administration. The Jaintia plains were regarded as the union territories of the Jaintias Union entirely under the control and supervision of the central authority. Indeed the whole Jaintia plains were regarded as the personnel estate of the Jaintia King where his direct personal rule prevailed in practice.

Before the evolution of the institution of the Kingship or Monarchy in Jaintia Hills, there existed a number of independent villages each under the control of the Langdoh (the priest) wielded power over the people. The priest exercised besides his religious function, civil and criminal functions as well. The Langdoh was at one time both the sacred and secular chief of the Jaintias. With the increase in the population and size of the territory (Raids or Elakas) consisting of a group of villages, secular functions also increased. This necessiated the bifurcation of sacred and secular functions. While the sacred function was retained by the Langdoh, that of secular function was then entrusted to an official called U Doloi. Again when the number of Doloiship increased, a feeling for unity arose among the Jaintias and this gave way to the growth of the institution of Kingship in Jaintia Hills. This system of administration ended with the coming of the British which then led to the still prevailing system of the Dolois, the Pators and the Waheh Chrangs as administrative heads of the three traditional political institutions in Jaintia Hills.

After Meghalaya became into a full-fledged state in 1972, the Khasi and the Jaintia Hills were constituted under one administrative unit but later it was changed when.District Council was introduced in the hill areas in 1952. Khasi and Jaintia Hills were put together but a separate District Council was created for each of these tribal groups.

JAINTIA IDENTITY:

It is believed that the original names of the Khasis is Kahii or Khahi. Despite their separate names of the Khasis and the Jaintias consider themselves as one and the same people. The word `Khasi' therefore always includes the Pnars.

The Pnars generally call the Khasis as Khynriam or Khasis to distinguish themselves as a distinct entity. The Khyriams on the other hand, call the Prans as Syntengs or Jaintia and refer to themselves as Khasis. Within the Khynriams group are the Bhois, the Wars and the Lyngams. Within the Pnar group are the Wars, the Nongtungs, the Lapangs, the Khynwangs, Nongphyllets. The Wars are thus found in both groups while they are usually known as War Jaintias or Wars Pnars. Due to political division between the Jaintias and the Khasis led to this differentiation between them which had existed throughout centuries.

According to Dr. Barister Pakam, "the word Syntang, in its turn was derived from the word "Sutnga" (Suteng), the ruling dynasty of the Jaintias, or from word "Sohkynting" (Smynting or Synting), a village through which the Khasis came to the Jaintia Hills." 1

According to Gurdon, "the Jaintia Hills took the name from the Raja of Jaintia"2. The religion, the Jaintias, their social habits, custom and prejudices .resemble those of the Khasis with the important exception of the large village of Nartiang where there is a Hindu temple dedicated to the Goddess Kali" 3

"The Jaintia Kingdom had a three-tier system of government. The Syiems, more often called Rajas, as they had converted to Hinduism, nominally ruled over the State. Succession was hereditary, passing from uncle to nephew. The Raja left the administration of the hill territory to twelve Dollois, while they resided in their capital Jaintiapur in the Syllet plains. In pre-colonial times the Dolois were obliged to remain in attendance for about six months in the year on the Jaintia Raja at Jaintiapur and Pators were appointed to act as their deputies during their absence. The only symbol of their allegiance to the Raja was an annual he goat from each of the villages under their administration which was mere symbolic." 4

In the matter of cohesion and solidarity the village community has became a significant Unit, a high level of organisation of linkages Matrilineal descent link in not significant factors beyond the scale of household level. Locality is more important in forming the socio-economic structure.

Religion in one of the factor which has an impact in, the Jaintia Society. Pnar religion is as ancient as the tribe itself. It is said `Pnar' or `Jaintia' is a Pnar because of his niam or religion, which regulates all his thoughts and activities. The Jaintia religion has both explicit and implicit functions in supporting political system and in bringing about social orders, cohesion, unity, continuity etc. The five web of Kinship lineage, ties, common residence, age set all unite people. Religion not only brings solidarity but cohesive sanction and helps in maintaining social orders. In the absence of written scripts, the moral principles have been guiding people. Rituals (Niam) represent unity and exclusiveness of the group. The Jaintias would have been unable to carry their collective life had their niam not guided them. The Jaintia social system is based on these niams and most of the values are common both for the non-Christians and the Christian Pnars.

In the Jaintia Society, it is found that village clustered around a particular area recognised themselves as a single political entity. If the components of a village cluster are physically adjacent, a village then appear to be as `Elaka' (province) of a single settlement. The political relationship between components villages in an `Elaka ` is unitary in style. The senior villager is an `Elaka' is the `Chief" or `Doloi'. A Doloi is elected from male members of the original clan (Kur) or clans. The original clan or clans are regarded as the earliest settlers and founders of the Illaka or Elaka. For this reason, these original clans have the privilege of setting up candidates for the office of Doloiship. A Doloi has his own respective `Elaka' and directly elected by the people of his Elaka and hold this office for the rest of his life and he is the axis of his people's political relation as well as their symbol of unity. But a Doloi may be punished, expelled or denounced if he aroused hostility by giving undue punishment or reward which is against the social norms. In such cases, people have the authority to strip the Doloi of his office. But all in all a Doloi is like a member of Parliament in the modern terminology. The social structures of the Jaintia people stretches beyond their political system and there are social relations between people of different Doloiship.

JAINTIA SOCIETY WHICH FOLLOWS THE MATRILINEAL SOCIETY

The Jaintia society is characterised by the matrilineal system. The Jaintias, like the Khasis, are divided into exogamous matrilineal clans (Kurs) whose members considers themselves to have descended from a common ancestress. In the Jaintia Hills the unit of the Jaintia system is the iiung (literally house of a family) which is composed of a grandmother, her daughter and their children. The clan consist of one common ancestor forming an exogamous group. Family (Ka iiung)' among the Jaintias is a socio-economic and religious unit.

Due to matrilocal residence, the structure of a Jaintia family assumes different forms. Family is the core of the Jaintia social organisation. Familiar kin, including the members of the sub-clan owes their development to the family. A member of the sub-clan (shi kpoh) is a secondary relative. Such a member can easily approach for any help from the family. Here, the constituent members are the grandmother, her daughter and their children but permanent residence consist of the youngest daughter (ka khadduh).

Normally the husbands do not go and live in his mother-in-law's house but only visits their wives. But with certain Pnars or Jaintias, this system is no longer observed. With the change of time, the marriage system is also changing among the Pnars.

In Meghalaya, among the matrilineal society - Pnars are quite different from the Khasis and the Garos. The Pnars are matrilineal and cross-cousin marriage is practised by them. The Pnars were firstly influenced by Hinduism but during British rule the waves of western culture influenced the Pnars. This change affected the socio-economic condition of the people. It is true that all men belong to their respective Kur or clan. To be more specific, they belong to their mothers. Some of the practices such as a man working his mother's house during the day and going to his wife's house at night still prevails.

In the matrilineal society where pervails cross cousin marriage, a man is related to women both as consanguines and affines. As a consanguines, they belong to the lineage and the clan of a women and as affines, they belong to other lineages and clans. As consanguines they are brothers and the sons of the women and as affines they are the husbands and fathers of their childrens. (though as father they are primary kin of the children of the women.)

The Pnar belong to their mother's house. The term `iiung' is also use for a household itself. The member of a house are strictly of matrilineal descendents who has a common right over the ancestral property, subject to a common authority and practice common rituals. The membership of the house comprises two persons - one holding authority and the other owning the property. A man continues to be a member of the same house all his life whether he marries or not. A woman if she is not the heiress that is, the youngest daughter will branch off after marriage though she will continue to be a member of her mother's house. The third generation from her will form an independent house. It is sometimes difficult to trace the clear line of each group as it is formed by the process of branching off.

The Jaintia trace their descent from female side and succession in their society takes place from the mother to the youngest living daughter. They follow the uxorilocal / matrilocal systems of residence. Different styles, however, could be found within the system of residence where the men after marriage have to move over to the house of their mother-in-law to stay with their wives. All the daughters, but the youngest one, have to move out of their mother's house with their husbands within a few years of their marriage if not immediately. Broadly speaking, two styles of marriage could be found in the society.

(i) Marriages through negotiations by the elders from both sides.
(ii) Marriages by self-choice.

In the first case, a boy and a girl may develop mutual liking for each other and may suggest their elders to take initiative in match making. Such marriages are ceremonialised ritually in the presence of their relatives and friends of the bridegroom and the bride. In the second case, that is, marriages by self choice, there is neither any involvement of elders from either side nor there is any religious celebrations.

In the Jaintia, inheritance of all property passes from mother to youngest daughter. The inheritance of the territorial rights, title and property will be confined to the children of the female members and the members of such groups is called matrilineal group, where children of the sisters are the members of the group but not the children of the brothers.

In the Jaintia society men have two options of house (iiung) to belong to-their mother or sister. After marriage, they may reside in the house of their mother of their wives or the house of their wives which they refer to iiung khon, that is, the house of their children. But the wife can claim this as her own house as it was set-up by her. The husband in the iiung has no importance as it is wife-centered. The descent group of the wife forms an independent unit which keeps itself distant from other official relation. In this system, wife has an important social position in comparison to the position of the husband. In the Jaintia family, the mother has a more prominent position than the father.

There are two identities of a family, that is, the mother as the creator, sustainer and container as well as the one who feeds the children. She is the legitimate owner of the children and has the natural claim and jurisdiction over her sons also. The son is expected to die in the mother's house. A Puza (slewnindi) has to be performed if the son dies in his wife's house. He belongs to the mother at all times even after death his bones should be preserved along with his mother's.

Among the Syntengs of Jaintia Hills, the system of inheritance prevalent is the same as that prevailing among the Khasis of the Khasi Hills but one major point, namely, succession to the self-acquired property of a male, there is a notable difference. The difference arises from the fact that, according to the Synteng system, the husband does not go and live in the house of his wife, but he visits his wife, though he remains in the house of his mother or female clans. It is his clan people who look after him in poverty or sickness and in times of troubles when he turns to them for help. The clan people are responsible for his cremation and have the supreme duty of placing his bones under the clan to save his spirit from wandering.

In case of jointly acquired property or joint earning, the clan people have no claim over the husband's labour on his wife property or land. As the earning of the husband during his stay with his wife belongs to his wife. At present, less importance is given to the clan people to the self acquired property of a male. The male now-a days also prefers to live with his wife rather than in the house of his mother. Among the Christians this has became the rule. In a number of cases, the husband and the wife live under the same roof together and earn jointly and acquire property. The wife in such cases bears the expenses of the death ceremony, and she along with her children inherit his self acquired property. If the wife undertakes not to remarry, she will inherit half of her husband's property which on her death will descend to her youngest daughter. The War Jaintias on the Southern side of the district are an exception to the rule. Both males and females own, control and possess property and also observe both the patrilineal and matrilineal custom. Alienable property cannot be disposed off without taking the consent of the members of the family including uncles and brothers. The custom of the youngest daughter inheriting the largest share continue till today.

Many non-Christian Pnar families makes a strong claim to the earning of the son. The son belongs to the mother but here also, he takes the position of an uncle. Christian Pnar husband is in the advantageous position because of the uxorilocal marriage. The husband stops visiting the wife's house after getting two or three children. After that, he lives separately iiaith his wife and children but visits his mother's house frequently.

Conclusion:

In the matrilineal set-up, women have a down dominant position because the succession rights of property belong to them. But women of Jaintia Hills do not enjoy equal rights with men in the affairs of secular institutions. Women even now also can neither exercise their right to vote in the election of dolois and Sardars nor can they contest in the election. Though the descent passes through the female lines, the married women in most respect are subordinate to their husbands.

Marriage and other relationships among the Jaintias are based on matrilineal systems, even then the male kin get due importance in the society. The balance between Maternal and Paternal are very much prevalent in the Jaintias society. Men enjoy dominant position in secular affairs whereas women occupy a privileged position in matters of property.

The Jaintia System is not matriarchal but matrilineal. Gradually the system is changing. Boys like to have independent houses and the authority of maternal uncles and brothers are becoming weak.

REFERENCES

1. Pakem, B., The Socio-Political System of the jaintia Tribe of Assam: An analysis of continuity and Change, Tribal Situation in India, Simla, 1972, p. 362.
2. Gurdon, P.R.T., The Khasis. London Macmillan, 1914, p-2
3. Mills, A.J.M., Report on the Khasi and Jaintia Hills. Calcutta, 1853 reprinted Shillong, 1901, pp. 5-6.
4. B. Pakem. cit. p. 353.

8

POPULATION GROWTH AND CHANGING DEMOGRAPHIC COMPOSITION IN JAINTIA HILLS DISTRICT, MEGHALAYA

Susmita Das and Sutapa Datta

Jaintia Hills, the easternmost district of Meghalaya, is located between 25° 2' N and 25° 45' latitude and 92° 5' E to 92° 45' E longitude. The average height of the district is 1200m, though the central part i.e., the Jowai Upland acts as an watershed between the river systems of the Brahmaputra valley and the Surma valley. However, the district as a whole has more flat lands than the adjoining East Khasi Hills District. The major rivers of the district are Myntdu (south flowing) and Kopili (north flowing). The natural vegetation covering the district is fairly dense accounting for about 35 percent of the total geographical area.

The district has a total population of 220473 persons (1991 census) with a density of 41 persons per sq. km. Of the total population 210558 are Scheduled Tribes indicating that the population is essentially tribal in nature (95.5 %). The growth rate of such population as has been observed by a number of geographers has shown a rapid change not only numerically but also in other related demographic patterns. However, the growth rate of population in Jaintia Hills (Jaintias) might have been affected in recent times due to a split brought in the otherwise common identity of Khasis as Khasis and Jaintias.

The growth of population in Jaintia Hills, as elsewhere in the state or for that matter in the entire north-eastern region, has shown a marked increase over the decades, particularly over the last three to four decades. Keeping parity with the change in population number, the entire demographic scenario of the district has changed in a fairly perceptible manner. The reflection of population growth, being positive or negative is quite marked on the demographic aspects of a population namely, gender ratio, agestructure, religious composition, literacy level and educational status, man-land ratio etc. An analysis of these aspects in terms of changing population numbers has significant bearing in any kind of population studies, and in understanding the man-environment relationships. It is in this backdrop that the present paper analyses the growth trend of population in Jaintia Hills along with its impact on certain demographic characteristics namely the male-female ratio, age-structure, religious and literacy composition. Casting a glance at the changing man-land ratio as appears from the population number and pattern of land utilisation in the district, the study also attempts to analyse the population environment relation in the area.

(1) Growth Rate i.e., $\frac{P_1 - P_2}{P_0}$ x 100

where r = growth rate

P_1 = Current year / decade population

P_0 = Previous year / decade population

DATA BASE: The paper is based on secondary data and the main sources are:

(i) Census of India
(ii) Basic Statistics of NER, NEC.
(iii) Data from concerned State Government Departments
(iv) Journals, Periodicals and Books.

The analysis in the paper is based on Community Development Block level data. But data being unavailable prior to 1981 for the same, the analysis has been restricted to 1981-91 information. However, as and when possible a larger span of time has also been considered.

The method used in the present work includes calculation of percentages and simple ratios.

ORGANISATION OF THE WORK:

The present work is organised in three smaller sections. Introducing the work and defining its limits in the first section is immediately followed by the first analytical section which deals with the growth trend of population in general on the one hand and that of the tribal population of the district on the other. The section also includes the factors explaining the existing patterns of growth in the district.

The next section deliberates the impact of general growth trend on selected demographic characteristics and end with an understanding of man-land ratio.

The final section of the work highlights the major findings of the study.

I

THE GROWTH TREND

The growth rate of population in the district of Jaintia Hills shows a pattern, which reflects two distinct phases. The first being upto the decade

1951, characterised by fluctuating trend and the second from 1961 onwards which reflect a spectacular increase and a steady rate of rise. The growth rate, has, however, more or less stabilized in the last two decades (Table-1).

Table-11 : **Decadal Growth Rate of Population in Jaintia Hills (1901-1991)**

Census Year	Total Population	Decadal Growth Rate (%)	Rural Population	Decadal Growth Rate (%)	Urban Popoulation	Decadal Growth Rate (%)
(1)	(2)	(3)	(4)	(5)	(6)	(7)
1901	35950	–	35950	–	–	–
1911	41783	16.23	41783	16.23	–	–
1921	43240	3.49	43240	3.49	–	–
1931	51524	19.18	51524	19.18	–	–
1941	59057	14.50	59057	14.50	–	
1951	64629	9.43	64629	9.43	–	
1961	82147	27.85	75950	27.85	6167	
1971	113562	38.24	104633	37.77	8929	44.79
1981	156402	37.72	143479	35.41	12923	44.73
1991	220473	40.97	199872	39.30	20601	59.41

Source: Census of India Series 16, Meghalaya.

A look at the rural-urban growth differentials of the district reveals that, while the growth rate of rural population is more or less similar with that of the general population, the urban areas marked a spectacular growth (Table-1). Moreover, the growth rate of urban population in Jaintia Hills is quite steady, contrary to the fluctuating trend as is marked in Meghalaya during the same period.

The growth rates of population at further lower level i.e., at the Community Development Block (C. D. Block) reveals a wide areal variation from 1981 to 1991 (Table-2). The growth rate is maximum in Thadlaskein C. D. Block while it is minimum in the Laskein C. D. Block. The other two C. D. Blocks i.e., Khliehriat and Amlarem shows a moderate rate of growth keeping parity more or less with the status average.

Table-12: **Decadal Growth Rate of Population in C.D. Blocks, Jaintia Hills (1981-91)**

C.D. Block	**Area**	**Population (1981)**	**Population (1991)**	**Decadal Growth (1981-91)**
Thadlaskiem	T	44709	78394	75.34
	R	31786	57793	81.82
	U	12923	20601	59.41
Laskeim	T	46853	46884	0.07
	R	46853	46884	0.07
	U	–	–	–

C.D. Block	Area	Population (1981)	Population (1991)	Decadal Growth (1981-91)
Khliehriat	T	43075	65228	51.43
	R	43075	65228	51.43
	U	–	–	–
Amlarem	T	21765	29967	37.68
	R	21765	29967	37.68
	U	–	–	–

Source: Census of India Series 1981 & 1991, Series 14 & 16 Meghalaya.

Table-13: **Decadal Growth Rate of Scheduled Tribe Population in Jaintia Hills, 1981-1991)**

C.D. Block	Area	Population (1981)	Population (1991)	Decadal Growth (1981-91)
JAINTIA HILLS	T	148710	210558	41.59
	R	137294	192043	39.88
	U	11416	18515	62.18
Thadlaskiem	T	42751	75825	77.36
	R	31335	57310	82.89
	U	11416	18515	62.18
Laskeim	T	46183	46551	0.80
	R	46183	46551	0.80
	U	–	–	–
Khliehriat	T	39775	61730	55.20
	R	39775	61730	55.20
	U	–	–	–
Amlarem	T	20001	26452	32.25
	R	20001	26452	32.25
	U	–	–	–

Source: Census of India Series 1981 & 1991, Series 14 & 16, Meghalaya.

The population composition of the district being essentially tribal is reflected in the growth pattern of the Scheduled Tribe (Table-3). The decadal variation of Scheduled Tribes from 1981-1991 again shows two extreme limits in Thadlaskein and Laskein C. D. Block and high rate of growth in the other two C. D. Blocks.

Factors of Growth:

The population growth in the district has taken place primarily due to the natural increase and to a small extent by immigration. In the absence of any data of natural birth (BR) and death (DR) rate for the district, the data on migration into the district is analysed to understand the rate and manner of natural growth.

A comparison of growth rate of population (total) in 1981-91 and that of the migrant population into the district (40.97% growth rate and -12.94% growth rate of migrants) justifies that the growth is largely due to the natural increase.

The spectacular growth in the decade 1951-61, which set the pattern of modern growth was due to an over all increase of the states total population which was again due to high natural increase (brought by a general improvement of health and medical facilities) on the one hand and due to the introduction of various developmental programmes on the other which led to movement of people from different areas into the state and the districts as well.

The C. D. Blocks reveal a marked variation in population growth. An abnormally high rise in Thadlaskein and an abrupt fall in Laskein is due to redistribution of villages between these two blocks (40 villages transferred from Laskein to Thadlaskein vide order from the Secy. to Govt. of Meghalaya C. D. No. CDD 31/82/13, dt. 25-Ol-85). This has also affected the growth of population in Khliehriat (5 villages transferred from Laskein) C. D. Block.

As regards the growth differential of rural and urban population, it can be stated that urban centre being only one in the district and also being recent in origin (should) as a rule, record a much higher growth than the rural population.

II

IMPACT OF POPULATION GROWTH

The growth of population whether due to natural increase or immigration is sure to bring some changes on the demographic character of any region or area and Jaintia Hills is no exception in this respect. The impact of population growth in the present work has been examined in terms of the following demographic aspects of Jaintia Hills.

A. SEX RATIO:

The sex ratio of Jaintia Hills shows a trend, which is slightly different from the state (Table-4). The ratio of female per 1000 male population shows a continuous decrease till the decade 1951. This at the context of a not so high and fluctuating growth rate of population suggests a general decline in the health and living condition of womenfolk in this area.

---

(2) The term sex-ratio in this work has been used to denote number of females per thousand males.

Table 14: **Sex Ratio of Jaintia Hills, Meghalaya and India (1901-1991)**

Census Year	Female per 1000 male		
	Jaintia Hills	Meghalaya	India
(1)	(2)	(3)	(4)
1901	1092	1036	972
1911	1064	1013	964
1921	1041	1000	955
1931	986	971	950
1941	967	966	945
1951	954	949	946
1961	1015	937	941
1971	999	942	930
1981	978	954	934
1991	973	955	927

Source: Census of India Series 1991, Series 16, Meghalaya.

The sudden rise in sex ratio in the decade 1961 indicates a general improvement in health and medical facilities following the Independence of the country. Moreover, very high ratio in Jaintia Hills and a sudden fall of sex ratio in the adjacent district of the East Khasi Hills in the same decade suggests an inter-district movement of females in the state being affected by the emergence of new urban centres.

The sex ratio is again observed to reduce from 1971 onwards and in the context of continuous rise in general population; this is explained as being a result of male selective immigration into the district.

B. Age Structure:

The impact of population growth on the age structure is better understood in terms of the dependency ratio[3] (Table-5). It is evident that the share of dependent population (0-14 and 60+) has increased over the decade from 49.7% in 1981 to 49.9% in 1991.

This inspite of being a marginal increase, its pressure on the working population should not be underestimated. This is further clarified from the percentage increase in the child population (0-6 years) over the last decade both among male and female population (Table-6). Such an increase in infant population is sure to create more pressure on the working population and the resultant economy.

Table-15: **Percentage Share of Dependent and Working Population**

Age-Group	**Percentate Population**					
	1981			**1991**		
	Person	**Male**	**Female**	**Person**	**Male**	**Female**
(1)	**(2)**	**(3)**	**(4)**	**(5)**	**(6)**	**(7)**
0-14	45.01	44.42	45.60	45.62	44.67	46.61
15-59	50.31	51.31	49.39	50.10	51.19	48.98
60+	4.69	4.69	5.01	4.28	4.15	4.41

Sources: Census of India Series 1981 & 1991, Series 14 & 16, Meghalaya.

(3) $DR = \frac{\text{No. of Persons in 0-14 \& 60 + Age group in a unit}}{\text{Total no. of person of the unit}} \times 100$

Table-16: **Age-Sex Structure of Population in Jaintia Hills (Total)**

Age-Group	Percentage Population			
	1981		1991	
	Male	Female	Male	Female
(1)	(2)	(3)	(4)	(5)
0 – 6	22.18	22.93	24.00	24.81
7 – 14	22.22	22.64	20.18	21.29
15 - 19	10.98	10.83	10.12	10.41
20 - 24	8.43	8.85	9.20	9.49
25 - 29	7.21	7.30	8.18	7.78
30 - 34	5.87	5.34	5.84	5.31
35 - 39	5.75	5.00	5.31	4.61
40 - 49	8.14	7.32	7.57	6.70
50 - 59	4.80	4.71	4.41	4.10
60 +	4.37	5.01	4.10	4.37
Age not stated	0.06	0.08	1.08	1.08

Source: Census of India Series 1981 & 1991, Series 14 & 16, Meghalaya.

Table-17: **Age-Sex Structure of Population in Jaintia Hills (Rural)**

Age-Group	Percentage Population			
	1981		1991	
	Male	Female	Male	Female
(1)	(2)	(3)	(4)	(5)
0 - 6	22.40	23.21	24.27	25.22
7 - 14	22.40	22.70	20.26	21.32
15 - 19	10.84	10.59	10.17	10.31
20 - 24	8.27	8.65	9.14	9.43
25 - 29	7.01	7.22	8.06	7.70
30 - 34	5.73	5.31	5.72	5.15
35 - 39	5.77	5.05	5.20	4.58

Age-Group	Percentage Population 1981		1991	
	Male	Female	Male	Female
(1)	(2)	(3)	(4)	(5)
40 - 49	8.21	7.37	7.55	6.74
50 - 59	4.88	4.78	4.48	4.15
60 +	4.41	5.04	4.21	4.43
Age not stated	0.06	0.06	0.95	0.98

Source: Census of India Series 1981 & 1991, Series 14 & 16, Meghalaya.

A look at the age-structure of both male and female population of the rural and urban areas of the district in the decade 1981-1991 (Table 7 & 8) reveals that there has been a considerable impact of coal mines in increasing the young adult age group population (15-29 years) in the rural areas. A decrease of urban population in the same age group indicates a growing tendency of inter-urban migration in connection with education, employment etc.

Table-18: **Age-Sex Structure of Population in Jaintia Hills (Urban)**

Age-Group	Percentage Population 1981		1991	
	Male	Female	Male	Female
(1)	(2)	(3)	(4)	(5)
0 - 6	19.64	19.79	21.40	20.87
7 - 14	20.18	21.92	19.41	21.04
15 - 19	12.51	13.54	9.66	11.33
20 - 24	10.18	10.99	9.81	10.56
25 - 29	9.40	8.18	9.32	8.55
30 - 34	7.39	5.63	7.00	6.92
35 - 39	5.51	4.42	6.39	4.99
40 - 49	7.38	6.77	7.77	6.36
50 - 59	3.81	3.93	3.72	3.55
60 +	3.96	4.59	3.13	3.80
Age not stated	0.14	0.23	2.39	2.04

Source: Census of India Series 1981 & 1991, Series 14 & 16, Meghalaya.

C. RELIGIOUS COMPOSITION:

The socio-demography of Jaintia Hills is also affected by the growth rate and growth related movement in a perceptible manner. Thus the religious composition of the two principal groups i.e. the Christians and the Hindus shows increase and decrease respectively over the period 1981-1991 in the district and its constituent C. D. Blocks as well. While rise in the Christian population is attributed to a natural increase and due to migration, the fall in Hindu population could possibly be due to out migration of nonindigenous population. Some amount of conversion of early Hindu Jaintias in the recent times may also be counted for a rise in Christian population. However, the fall in the percentage of tribal religion over the decade 1981-91 is considered as the most probable reason for rise in the Christians (Table-9).

Table-19: **Changing Composition of Religious Groups in Jaintia Hills (1981-1991)**

Religious Group	Jaintia Hills		Thadlaskein		Laskein		Khliehriat		Amlarem	
	1981	1991	1981	1991	1981	1991	1981	1991	1981	1991
(1)	(2)	(3)	(4)	(5)	(6)	(7)	(8)	(9)	(10)	(11)
Christians	55.93	62.72	56.57	64.58	55.35	56.13	60.12	66.02	47.58	61.02
Hindus	5.98	4.47	7.31	3.88	1.86	0.92	7.52	7.25	9.11	5.46
Muslims	0.11	0.33	0.18	0.19	0.01	0.002	0.18	0.80	0.06	0.14
Buddhists	0.04	0.002	0.12	---	---	---	0.01	0.01	0.01	0.06
Sikhs	0.01	0.001	0.02	---	---	0.002	0.03	0.03	0.01	---
Jains	---	0.01	----	0.02	---	0.002	---	---	---	---
Other Religion & Persuation	37.87	32.46	37.79	31.29	42.75	42.93	32.07	32.07	43.13	33.40
Religion not stated	0.04	0.02	0.02	0.04	0.03		0.06	0.06	0.10	---

Source: Census of India Series 1981 & 1991, Series 14 & 16, Meghalaya.

There has been an increase, however, insignificant may be in the percentage of Muslim population in the district. This is an indication of immigration then across the border from the neighbouring country Bangladesh. The higher increase in this group in the two blocks of Khliehriat and Amlaren (along Bangladesh border) further justifies the above observation.

D. LITERACY RATE AND EDUCATIONAL LEVEL:

The rate of literacy in Jaintia hills shows more or less a uniform trend of growth along its areal units (C.D. Blocks). Keeping parity with the general increase in population, the rate of literacy has also increased (Table-10).

Table-20: **Changing Literacy Composition in Jaintia Hills (1981 - 1991)**

Districts / C. D. Block	Area	Percentage of Literacy					
		1981			1991		
		Person	Male	Female	Person	Male	Female
(1)	(2)	(3)	(4)	(5)	(6)	(7)	(8)
JAINTIA	T	24.51	24.63	24.38	26.70	26.12	27.30
HILLS	R	20.77	20.56	20.98	22.84	21.99	22.71
	U	66.01	70.17	61.83	64.17	66.29	62.00
Thadlaskiem	T	32.86	32.54	33.17	32.06	31.16	32.96
	R	19.38	17.02	21.69	20.62	18.34	22.85
	U	66.01	70.17	61.83	64.17	66.27	62.00

Districts / C. D. Block	Area	Percentage of Literacy 1981 Person	Male	Female	1991 Person	Male	Female
(1)	(2)	(3)	(4)	(5)	(6)	(7)	(8)
Laskeim	T	19.82	18.10	21.53	22.39	19.08	25.67
	R	19.82	18.10	21.53	22.39	19.08	25.67
	U	–	–	–	–	–	–
Khliehriat	T	19.37	20.91	17.65	21.36	22.64	19.96
	R	19.37	20.91	17.65	21.36	22.64	19.96
	U	–	–	–	–	–	–
Amlarem	T	27.59	30.20.	24.97	31.06	31.77	30.31
	R	27.59	30.20	24.97	31.06	31.77	30.31
	U	–	–	–	–	–	–

Source: Census of India, 1981 & 1991, Series 14 & 16, Meghalaya.

However, a look into the rural-urban literacy differentials bring out that, though rural literacy rate has increased from 20.77 percent in 1981 to 22.84 percent in 1991, but urban literacy rate surprisingly has decreased from 66.01 percent to 64.17 percent over the same period. This becomes more conspicoous when the literacy rate of male and female population in urban areas are considered. Though the urban population in the district and its constituent C. D. Blocks registered a marked increase, the fall of urban male literates in this context highlights certain social conditions, which are being presumably surfaced in recent time. One of this could be the moving out of a considerably large section of urban male literates outside the district in connection with higher education, better employment and so on.

The analysis of literacy rate at different levels of education for rural and urban areas could have thrown more lights in this respect. But in the absence of correct data, this could not be carried out in the present work.

D. Man-Land Ratio:

The impact of population growth in the district is also reflected on the man-land ratio. Though the land utilization statistics of the district over the show an increase in cultivable land it is quite insignificant compared to the absolute increase in population. Thus, while the cultivable area has increased by only two percent over the decade 1981-91, the increase in population has been almost 40 percent in the same period. Such a disproportionate rate of growth of population and cultivable land clearly indicates that the man-land ratio in the district is becoming increasingly critical. This is further exemplified in Table-11 showing average rural[4], agricultural[5] and physiological[6] densities in the district and its constituent C. D. Blocks as well as their pattern of change: It appears that the agricultural and physiological densities of the district, which are much higher than the average density, indicate that increase in population number is creating excessive pressure on the agricultural sector in the district.

Table-21: **Density of Population in Jaintia Hills (1981-1991)**

C.D. Block	Density of Population							
	Average		Rural		Agricultural		Physiological	
	1981	1991	1981	1991	1981	1991	1981	1991
(1)	(2)		(3)		(4)		(5)	
JAINTIA HILLS	41	58	38	52	184	226	486	672
Thadlaskein	70	104	50	78	—	—	—	—
Laskein	65	85	55	85	—	—	—	—
Khliehriat	21	31	21	31	—	—	—	—
Amlarem	55	75	55	75	—	—	—	—

Source: Census of India 1981 & 1991, Series 14 & 16, Meghalaya, and Land Utilisation Statistics 1980-81 & 1990-91 record, Directorate of Economics and Statistics, Govt. of Meghalaya.

Moreover, it is also noticed that the number of agricultural labourer is on the rise in the recent decades. These together indicate a general decrease in the amount of land holding (in the context of increasing growth) as well as restricting people's access to land (in the context of increasing agricultural labourer).

III

FINDINGS AND CONCLUSION

The analysis carried out so far highlights certain broad characteristics as regards the population growth and demographic composition in Jaintia Hills.

The growth rate of population in the district has been very high particularly from 1961 onwards. Such a high growth rate of population is largely due to natural increase, which is indicated by a high rate of population growth, large share of child population and a negative rise in migrant population.

Inspite of the high growth rate of population in the district, its constituent units do not reflect a very uniform pattern of growth. The growth rate is exceptionally high in Thadlaskein C. D. Block and very low in Laskein C. D. Block. This highly uneven growth rate has been primarily affected by the redistribution of the villages among the C. D. Blocks.

4. Rural Density $= \dfrac{\text{Total Rural Population of a unit}}{\text{Total Rural Area of the unit}}$

5. Agricultural Density $= \dfrac{\text{Total population of a unit}}{\text{Net sown area of the unit}}$

6. Physiological Density $= \dfrac{\text{Total Population of a unit}}{\text{Net sown Area of the unit}}$

As regards the growth rates among rural and urban areas, it is observed that though the rural areas reflects more or less the same pattern as that with the total population, the urban growth rate is quite high in the district. This high urban growth rate is attributed to a relatively recent creation of the only urban centre of the district.

As far as the growth rate of tribal population is concerned it shows-more or less the similar pattern with he total population of the district. Here again the blocks of Thadlaskein and Laskein show the two extreme conditions.

Sex-ratio in the district is observed to have a direct relation with the growth pattern of population at different phases being effected by the prevailing health and medical conditions, intra-district migration and immigration which has been specifically male selective. However; the most positive aspect in this regard is that sex-ratio has remained higher in the district then the state.

The age structure and composition of rural and urban population in the district show fairly different trends. This trend while being affected by out migration from the urban areas is possibly due to immigration in the different organised and unorganized sector of rural areas.

The impact of growth of population on religious composition is particularly reflected on the groups of Christians, Hindus and Tribal and Indigenus religions, being affected by both conversion and migration. The only other religious group reflecting different type of change is the Muslims, which is primarily due to immigration from across the border.

Though literacy rate has increased in the district marginally but compared to the rise in population such an increase is negligible. However, the rate of increase in literacy is not uniform among the rural and urban population, which is caused by low male literacy of the urban population.

The high population growth rate has made the man-land ratio quite critical. As people of Jaintia Hills depend primarily on agrarian economy, such critical man-land ratio is deteriorating the agrarian base of the district. This is realized in view of the increasing number of agricultural labourer along with a fall in the number of cultivators.

The major findings of the study as highlighted in the previous paragraphs, lead us to conclude that the population growth rate in the district is not only high, but it is quite disproportionate among the various social groups and areal units. This, in view of not so suificient resource base is bound to reduce the rate of and scope for socio-economic development in the district. It also appears from the social qualities of population and their pattern, that the rate of human resource development is also not very high. Thus, more than emphasizing on a check of the growth of population, what is more urgently needed is an overall development of the quality of population. This can ensure an enhancement in the pace of socio-economic development as well as an improvement of the total environment of Jaintia Hills in Meghalaya.

REFERENCES

1. Ahmed (ed), Aijazuddin, et. al. (1997): Demographic Transition: The Third world Scenario, Rawat Publications, New Delhi.
2. Bhakta, G. P. (1992): Geography of North East India, Akashi Book Depot, New Delhi. Census of India (1981): Series 14, Meghalaya, Primary Census Abstract.
3. Census of India (1991): Series 16, Meghalaya, Primary Census Abstract.
4. Raja, Mooniz et. al. (1976): Tribal Population of India, Spatial Pattern of Clustering and Concentration, in All India Symposium on Tribal Demography in India, Imphal, Manipur.
5. Nath, Alakananda (1986): Demographic Changes among Scheduled Tribes - 1961-1981, in Datta Ray, B. (ed), The Pattern and Problems of Population in North East India, Uppal Publishing, New Delhi.
6. Datta, Sutapa (1996): Socio-Economic Structure of Urban Khasi Population in Meghalaya with special reference to Shillong Urban Agglomeration: A Geographical Analysis, Unpublished Ph.D Thesis, Gauhati University, Guwahati.

9

POPULATION DYNAMICS OF JAINTIA HILLS DISTRICT OF MEGHALAYA

Debashis Basu

In the present century the talks of any developmental planning, programmes and policies of the society towards a better livelihood are converging to the population and its growth which is receiving more mileage than in the yester years. Population can be studied in the view of 'static aspect' visualising an instantaneous picture of a community at a particular point of time and the 'Dynamic aspects' which provides information's pertaining to the trends of population characteristics. With the help of this population census data some administative purposes in the form of developmental plans programmes, and policies regarding socio-economic aspects encompassing education, health, food, basic facilities are usually accomplished. In continuation with the all round socio-economic betterment of the society, the approaches usually suggest to formulate the development in such a way so as to have both short term as well as longterm perspectives.

In the present paper an attempt has been made to discuss the population and its growth trend during the period between 1901 and 1991 in the Jaintis Hills district of Meghalaya. The data utilised here are taken from the Cencus of India, 1991 Basic Statistics of North Eastern Region 1995. The above aspect of population is expressed with percentage decadel variation and continuous version of the exponential growth formula (i.e., percentage exponential growth of population between two census years) with reference to the state of Meghalaya.

POPULATION GROWTH

In the district of Jaintia Hills in the Meghalaya the population has been increasing steadily with the increase of total population of India in general and the state Meghalaya in particular. In table 2 it shows that the population figures of total and gender wise population in the Jaintia Hills district between 1901 and 1991 percentage decadel variation increases steadily. Till 1951 the population increases with a percentage decadel variation below 20.00 but 1951 onwards the sharp acceleration of population's increase is observed. During the period between 1961 and 1991 the percentage decadel variation in the Jaintia Hills district is marked with the range from 27.11 to 40.97. The appreciable increase of the population in the same district after 1951 may be attributed to a large extent of *migration* from the neighboring areas. Unfortunately the data on migration in the Jaintia Hills district is not available, but as a whole, as Srivastava (1987:61) that the Meghalaya state is the second largest state interms of migrants in absolute terms after the Tripura's and to some extent, the availability of modern medicine system plays an important role. Table 1 shows the disease pattern in the Jaintia Hills district. It indicates that number of deaths during the years shows a decrease of death to a greater extent. This is assumed as the effect of modern treatment.

In Table 3 it shows that Exponential annual growth rate (percent) of the population in the Jaintia Hills district, *1901-1991*. It may be noted that census data for urban population of Jaintia Hills district are not available till 1951-1961 period.

The annual growth rate of the population of this district in the successive periods till 1991 are calculated with the help of continuous version of the exponential growth formula. The formula is as follows:

$$g = \text{Log}\,(P_t / P_o)\ 100 / t$$

Where giis the percentage annual exponential growth rate of the population between two census years, and Log denotes natural logarithm to the bases,

P_t = Population of the latter census
P_o – Population of the previous census
t = The number of years (ten) between the censuses'

The right hand side of the formula is multiplied for percentage.

Following observations based on the table showing the annual growth rate (percent) for the population genderwise in the rural, urban, district and state levels, are observed:

i) The range of annual growth rate for the male is between 0.47 in 1911-21 and 2.09 in 1951-61; and the range in the latter stage, is between 3.32 in 1961-71 and 3.46 in 1981-91. The *annual* growth rates for the female varies from 0.24 in 1911-21 to 2.71 in 1951-61; while in the latter stage it varies from 3.10 in 1971-81 to 3.40 in 1981-91.

ii) The *annual* growth rates observed during the period between 1901 and 1991 are in two stages of growth patterns. In the rural population in this district, the annual growth rates are observed with moderate fractuations in the range between 0.34 in 1911-12 and 1.75 in 1921-31;

while in the latter stage the annual growth rates varies from 3.16 in 1971-81 to 3.31 in 1981-91.

iii) In between two periods from 1901-11 to 1951-61 the census data for the population in the urban areas in this district are not available. In the corresponding stage the annual growth rates varies from 3.70 in 1961-71 to 4.66 in 1981-91.

iv) In this district itself the annual growth rate patterns follow the same trend as observed in the former cases and so the trend in the state too.

Tanking the annual growth rate patterns in the two stages for the different former populations into consideration, it is observed that the values of the same are higher than those of values in the state. And in precise, the annual growth rate values in the latter stage increased with moderate intensity.

SEX RATIO

The census, of India is used the word 'sex ratio' to describe the number of females per 1000 males in any particular population. The probable sex ratio at birth is between 960 and 930 (Mitra, 1978).

In Table for sex ratio there is a steady deterioration from 1092 in 1901 to 954 in 1951 and again from 1015 in 1951 to 973 in 1991. In 1961 the sex ratio being 1015, the highest value during the period between 1961 and 1991 may be attributed to the *migration* from the neighboring areas. In the later periods the value of the sex ratio steadily decreases. This phenomenon of having lower sex ratio in the successive periods may be attributed to the *higher female infant mortality* rate as compared to that of male infant mortality rate. More demographic study in this regard can help.

RURAL – URBAN POPULATION

Usually population growth is contributed by rural and urban population components and their growth. In the *Table 4* for rural and urban populations, it shows that the rural population in the Jaintia Hills district is observed with higher proportion of the total population. In the context of urban and rural population composition, it is well known that the areas fulfilling some criteria termed as urban areas which are characterised with some developmental features. These urban areas are charactrised with low birth rate. In the Jaintia Hills district the population in the urban areas are observed with higher exponential annual growth rate as compared to that of rural population, which in turn, shows that unlike the development characterised by low birth rate having been positively correlated with urbanisations, the urban population in the Jaintia Hills district is observed with higher exponential annual growth rate as compared to those in the rural areas which reveals that the extent of urbanisation in the urban areas is not so at per with the other parts of the country in general, and the state in particular, or in other words, it *may advocate* the larger extent of migration from rural areas in to the urban areas. But in this case (in the Jaintia Hills district) both the factors, i.e. the poor extent of urbanisation an the migration from the rural areas in to the urban areas play significant role, which in turn, also supports the view of Prof. Taher, is that "what is happening in the name of urbanisation in this district, is infact, ruralisation of urban settlements.

ACKNOWLEDGEMENT

The author expresses his sincere gratitude to Prof. B. Dutta Ray, Secretary, NEICSSR, Dr. (Mrs) Gitasree Das, Deptt. Of Statistics, NEHU, and Dr. (Mrs) I. Blah, Director, Directorate of Health Services (MCH & FW), Govt. of Meghalaya for their kind encouragement.

Table-22 : Disease Pattern in the Jaintia Hills District during 1995 – 2000

S. No	Name of Diseases	1995-96		1996-97		1997-98		1998-99		1999-2000	
		Cases	Death	Cases	Death	Cases	Death	cases	Death	Cases	Death
1.	Acute Diarrhoeal	3554	16	6691	16	9103	13	13455	14	12586	6
2.	Pneumonia/ ARI	75	-	6617	4	3490	-	2975	-	6250	4
3.	Measles	554	4	245	-	377	1	448	1	465	8
4.	Diptheria	-	-	1	-	-	-	-	-	1	-
5.	Whooping Cough	-	-	-	-	-	-	-	-	8	-

Sources: Office of the Director of Health Services (MCH & FW) Government of Meghalaya

Table-23 : Population Trend in the Jaintia Hills District of Meghalaya

Year	Total Persons	Decade Variation	Percentage Decade Variation	Male	Female
1901	35,950	-	-	17,181	18,769
1911	41,783	5,833	16.23	20,212	21,541
1921	43,240	1,457	3.49	21,186	22,054
1931	51,534	8,294	19.18	25,949	25,585
1941	59,057	7,523	14.60	30,026	29,031
1951	64,629	5,572	9.43	33,077	31,552
1961	82,147	17,518	27.11	40,760	41,387
1971	113,562	31,415	38.24	56,810	56,752
1981	156,402	42,840	37.72	79,052	77,350
1991	220,473	64,071	40.97	111,753	108,720

Sources : Cencus of India, 1991. General Population Tables and Primary Cencus Abstract; Meghalaya, B. Series – 16. Part II – A&B

Table – 24 : Progress in Urban and Rural Population on State / District 1901- 1991

State/ Dist	1901	1911	1921	1931	1941	1951	1961	1971	1981	1991
					Urban Population					
Megh	9621	13639	17203	25536	38192	58512	117483	147170	241333	330047
J. Hills	-	-	-	-	-	-	6167	8929	12923	20601
					Rural Population					
Megh	330903	380366	405200	454301	517628	547162	651897	864529	1094486	1444731
J. Hills	35950	41783	43240	51534	59057	64629	79550	104633	143479	199872

Census of India, Part II – A&B, Series – 16, Meghalaya

Table-25 : Exponential Annual Growth Rate (Percent) of Population in the Jaintia Hills, 1901 – 1991

Period	Male	Female	Rural	Urban	Dist / J. Hills	State Meghalaya
1901-11	1.62	1.32	1.50	NA	1.50	1.44
1911-21	0.47	0.24	0.34	NA	0.34	0.69
1921-31	2.03	1.49	1.75	NA	1.75	1.31
1931-41	1.46	1.26	1.36	NA	1.36	1.45
1941-51	0.97	0.83	0.90	NA	0.90	0.86
1951-61	2.09	2.71	1.61	NA	2.40	2.38
1961-71	3.32	3.16	3.20	3.70	3.24	2.75
1971-81	3.30	3.10	3.16	3.70	3.20	2.78
1981-91	3.46	3.40	3.31	4.66	3.43	2.84

Table – 26 : Density of Population in 1981 and 1991

State / District	Density of Population per sq. km. 1981	1991
Meghalaya	60	79
Jaintia Hills	41	58

Census of India, 1991

Table-6 : Sex Ratio 1901 – 1991

State/ District	1901	1911	1921	1931	1941	1951	1961	1971	1981	1991
Meghalaya	1036	1013	1000	971	966	949	937	942	954	955
Jaintia Hills	1092	1064	1041	986	967	954	1015	999	978	973

Census of India, 1991

REFERENCES

1. Mitra, A. 1978 *India's Population: Aspects of Quality and Control.* Vol. 1. Family Planning Foundation/ICSSR. Abhinava Publications, New Delhi
2. Srivastava, S.C. 1987 *Demographic Profile of North East India.* Mittal Publications, Delhi.

10

SOCIO-ECONOMIC DIMENSIONS OF POPULATION IN JAINTIA HILLS DISTRICT, MEGHALAYA

Madhushree Das Kar
Bimal K. Kar

INTRODUCTION

Meghalaya, one of the tribal dominated states in India's north-east, is lagging behind many other parts of the country in demographic and socio-economic fronts. Among the north-eastern states also, the state of Meghalaya in this context does not occupy a satisfactory position. The situation is even more discouraging in the district of Jaintia Hills. The population growth rate in the district has been found to be quite high during the last few decades. The prevailing higher rates of population growth have resulted in the increase of percentage share of population in the district. It may, however, be mentioned here that in spite of the influence of Christianity, the district still socio-economically lags behind most of the districts in the North East.

With the above perspectives in mind, an attempt is made in this paper to outline the demographic and socio-economic characteristics of population in the district using secondary data drawn from the Census of India and other government reports.

The parameters like population growth rate, fertility rate, proportion of population in the age groups 0-6 and 0-14, mean female age at marriage, urbanisation, literacy rate, work participation rate, and occupational composition are considered here.

THE STUDY AREA

With in area 3819 km^2 and a population of 2,20,473 (as per a 991 census) the district of Jaintia Hills accounts for 17.03 per cent and 12.42 per cent of the state's respective totals. From the relief point of view, the district presents a hilly and rugged topography. The district consists of four Community Development (CD) blocks, viz. Thadlaskein, Laskein, Khliehriat and Amlarem. The district has a rich forest cover ranging from tropical to temperate. The Narpuh and Saipung reserved forests occupy the southern part of the district. The settlement pattern is very dispersed due to its rugged terrain condition and dense forest cover. Hamletted settlements are also very common in the district. The major settlements are located either along the road or river. The density of population in the district is as low as 58 as against the state average of 79 persons per km^2. Urbanization, which is confined to only Thadlaskein CD block in the district, is found to be as low as 9.34 per cent as against 18.60 per cent in the state. It may be mentioned here that constituting about 90 per cent of the population the tribals from the majority in the district. Of the total population again, the Christians, and the other religions and persuasion constitute 55 per cent and 38 per cent respectively.

The economy of the district is primarily based on the primary sector comprising agriculture, forestry and mining. The northern part of the district has a good network of surface roads. Most of the important places in the northern part are connected with NH44 and other motorable roads. But the southern part is still backward in terms of surface road or communication.

POPULATION GROWTH

The population growth rate in the Jaintia Hills district has always been found to be higher than the state's average during the last few decades. After independence, during the period 1951-1991, the population of the district has increased 3.4 times (from 65,000 in 1951 to 220,000 in 1991) as against 2.9 times in the state (from 6 lakhs in 1951 to 17.7 lakhs in 1991). Strikingly, during the last decade (1981-91) the population growth became as high as 40.96 per cent in the district as against 32.86 per cent in the state (Table 1). Such a high growth rate of population is primarily associated with the prevalence of high birth rate in the district. The growth rate would have been even higher had there been no migration to the capital city of Shillong. As a consequence of the prevailing higher growth rates the percentage share of population in the district has increased from 10.67 per cent in 1951 to 12.42 per cent in 1991. If the growth of population still continues at such a high rate, the population in the district is likely to cross the 3-lakh mark in the early part of 2001.

Table–27 : Population Growth in Meghalaya and Jaintia Hills during 1901-1991

Year	Meghalaya	Percentag Growth of Population	Jaintia Hills	Percentage Growth of Population	Percentage Share of Population
1901	340,524	-	35,950	-	10.56
1911	394,005	15.71	41,783	16.23	10.60
1921	422,403	7.21	43,240	3.49	10.24

Year	Meghalaya	Percentag Growth of Population	Jaintia Hills	Percentage Growth of Population	Percentage Share of Population
1931	480,837	13.83	51,534	19.18	10.72
1941	555,820	15.59	59,057	14.60	10.63
1951	605,674	8.97	64,629	9.43	10.67
1961	769,380	27.03	82,147	27.11	10.68
1971	1,011,699	31.50	113,562	38.24	11.22
1981	1,335,819	32.04	156,402	37.72	11.71
1991	1,774,778	32.86	220,473	40.96	12.42

Source : Portrait of Population of Meghalaya, Census of India, 1981 and Primary Census Abstract of Meghalaya, Census of India, 1991.

So far the population growth within the district is concerned it is quite uneven. The growth during 1981-1991 was found to be as high as 75.34 per cent in Thadlaskein, followed by 51.43 per cent in Laskein. Such a noticeably high degree of variation in population growth among the CD blocks is certainly the result of inter CD block migration and change in block boundary. It may be mentioned here that 40 villages had been carved out from Laskein block to Thadlaskein block during the period 1981-1991. As a result, the growth rates of population became as high as 75.34 per cent in the Thadlaskein block and as low as 0.06 per cent in Laskein block during the said period. Further, the extent of migration from Laskein block to the urbanised Thadlaskein block has also not been so insignificant. Such a significant variation in population growth, on the other hand, indirectly reveals that the economic base of the Thadlaskein and Khliehriat CD blocks are relatively better than the other two blocks.

DEMOGRAPHIC CHARACTERISTICS

Demographically speaking, the district of Jaintia Hills occupies a discouraging position in the whole state of Meghalaya. Although the adjusted crude birth rates are found to be as high as 44.65 in the district and 44.83 in the state, the infant mortality rates (IMR) are found to be 61 and 80 respectively. The prevailing low IMR in the district as compared to the state average results in high natural growth of population in the district. This phenomenon is also reflected in its high proportion in the age group 0-6 (24.40 per cent as against 22.18 per cent in the state) and 0-14 (44.30 per cent as against 42.23 per cent in the state). Besides, the total fertility rate is also found to be higher in the district (6.86) than in the state (6.33). The relatively lower mean female age at marriage in the district (19.1) as compared to the state average (19.3) is also to a certain extent indicative of the prevailing high fertility rate in the district (Table 2). All these demographic conditions have been responsible for the prevalence high annual exponential growth rate of population in the district. On the other hand, considerably high sex ration (973) shows that volume of migration into the district has been insignificant.

Table – 28 : Comparative Characteristics of Population of Meghalaya and Jaintia Hills

S. No	Population Characteristics	Jaintia Hills	Meghalaya
1.	Percentage of Population in Age Group 0-6	24.40	22.18
2.	Crude Birth Rate (per thousand)	44.65	44.83
3.	Total Fertility Rate	6.86	6.33
4.	Infant Mortality Rate	61.00	80.00
5.	Percentage of Population in Age Group 0-14	44.30	42.23
6.	Mean Female Age at Marriage	19.10	19.30
7.	Percentage of Urban Population	9.34	18.60
8.	Annual Exponential Growth Rate (in per cent)	3.43	2.84
9.	Sex Ratio	973.00	955.00

Source : Census of India, 1991.

SOCIO-ECONOMIC CHARACTERISTICS

Being composed of as high as 89.87 per cent of tribal population of district of Jaintia Hills presents a homogeneous social character. In respect of religious composition also the district's population is largely constituted by the Christians and tribal religion (together 93.80 per cent). It may be mentioned here that although the Christians form the majority in the district, there has been hardly any significant impact in changing the socio-economic condition in most parts of the district. In terms of literacy rate also, the district (35.32 per cent) occupies a discouraging position as compared to the state as a whole (49.10 per cent). Within the district again, literacy rate is found to be as low as 28.06 per cent in Khilehriat block and as high as 42.15 per cent in the urbanised Thadlaskein block (Table 3). It is worth mentioning here that although the literacy rate on the whole is quite low, the impact of matriliny is well reflected in the gender equality in literacy almost throughout the district. It is striking enough to note that the female literacy rates in Laskein and Thadlaskein blocks are higher than their male counterparts. This is also true in the case of the district as a whole. The lack of adequate educational facilities combined with poverty and lack of consciousness towards education is largely responsible for low educational development in the whole district.

Table-29 : CD Block-wise Literacy, Work Participation and Occupational Composition in Jaintia Hills District, Meghalaya, 1991

Sl. No.	CD Block	Literacy Rate		Work Participation		Occupational Composition		
		Male	Female	Male	Female	Primary	Secondary	Tertiary
1.	Thadlaskein	40.97	43.32	50.76	39.34	72.36	3.05	24.59
2.	Laskein	25.90	34.74	50.53	38.17	86.67	1.27	12.06
3.	Khliehriat	29.38	20.67	55.91	43.61	84.82	0.94	14.24
4.	Amlarem	41.48	40.10	53.43	37.43	68.24	8.87	22.89
	Jaintia Hills	34.37	36.31	52.65	40.05	78.74	2.76	18.50
	MEGHALAYA	53.12	44.85	50.07	34.93	74.80	3.74	21.46

Source : Primary Census Abstract of Meghalaya, 1991, Directorate of Census Operations, Meghalaya, Shillong.

The prevailing rugged hilly terrain and available forest and mineral resources to a great extent determine the economy of the district. The overall work participation rate is found to be as high as 46.44 per cent in the district as against 42.67 per cent in the state. Within the district again, the participation rate varies from as low as 44.31 per cent in Laskein block to as high as 50.04 per cent in Khilehriat block (Table 3). The work participation rate is also quite high among the females in the district (40.05 per cent) due to the practice of jhuming and female mobility. Accordingly, about three-fourth of the total main workers in the district are found to be engaged in the primary sector. It is quite discouraging to note that about one-fourth of the total main workers alone in the Amlarem block are engaged as agricultural labourers. Satisfactorily, however, the proportions of workers in the secondary and tertiary sectors are found to be considerably high in the Amlarem and Thadlaskein blocks. Truly speaking, at the present mode of production there is altogether limited scope for the expansion of economy in other sectors.

CONCLUSION

In conclusion, the overall picture of demographic and socio-economic dimensions of population in the district found to be far from satisfactory as compared to the state scenario. The whole scenario of demographic and socio-economic backwardness in the district has been largely associated with the lack of socio-economic and infrastructure development. The prevailing poverty and lack of consciousness among a large segment of the rural population is no less important factor in this respect. It is, therefore, high time to take necessary and effective measures to initiate the sustainable development programmes throughout the district.

REFERENCES

1. Census of India (1981) : A Portrait of Population of Meghalaya, Directorate of Census Operations, Meghalaya, Shillong.
2. Census of India (1988) : Regional Divisions of India – A Cartographic Analysis, Series I, Vol. XIV, Meghalaya.
3. Census of India (1991) :District Level Estimates of Fertility and Child Mortality for 1991 and their Inter Relations with other Variables, Occasional Paper No. 1 of 1997.
4. Census of India (1991) : Primary Census Abstract of Meghalaya, Directorate of Census Operations, Meghalaya, Shillong.

11

JAINTIA KINGDOM: ITS ROLE AND IMPACT OF BRITISH COLONIALISM

R.P. Athparia
D.N. Pandey

I

The name "Jaintia Hills" has been in use since the area came under the British Rule in 1835. The name was used to differentiate it from the plain areas of the old Jaintia Kingdom, the capital of which was Jaintiapur. The whole of this area is now in Bangladesh. Suniti Kumar Chatterjee suggests that the name Jaintia has been derived from the name "Synteng" by which the people of the Jaintia Hills used to call themselves (C.F. Simon, I.M. 1995:1). Bhuyan (1937) opines that the name Jaintia derives from the goddess Jayanti Devi, one of the deities worshipped by the royal family of the Jaintia Kingdom when they were converted to Hinduism, probably in the 16th century, after the consolidation of their sway over the plains tracts in the south.

The present Jaintia Hills is the eastern most district of Meghalaya. It is bounded by the Karbi Anglong district in the north; the North Cachar Hills to the east; Bangladesh to the South and East Khasi Hills district to the West. The total area of the district is 3819 sq. kms. With a population of 1,56,402 according to 1981 census. Out of the total population, 79,052 are males and 77,350 females. The density of population is 46.49 persons per sq.km.

The Jaintia Hills district constituted the nucleus from which the Jaintia Kingdom eventually developed. The Jaintia Kingdom was the largest and most prosperous covering not only the Jaintia Hills but also considerable tracts of both Assam and Surma Valleys. Pakem (1977) states that the institution of Jaintia Kingdom appeared to have been in existence as early as the fifth century B.C. when a Jaintia royal embassy was reported to have visited China. Both Gassah (1989) and Pakem (1977) studied independently the political institutions of the jaintia and its courses of development since pre Independence time. They stated that the institution of Jaintia Kingdom was a three-tier system of administration. It was firmly established in Ri-Jaintia. At the top, there was the king (U syiem or Rajah). In the middle level, there were provinces (Raid or Illakas) each under a provincial governor (U Doloi) and at the bottom, there was a village chief or headman (U Wahehchnong) in every village. Occasionally, an extra tier between the Province and the village was instituted whenever the province was extra ordinarily large. Such an extra tier was usually placed under the charge of U Pator.

II

Originally, the Jaintia Kingship confined to the hill tracts. The ruling family that the Sutnga claimed supernatural origin. The off spring of an union between a mortal man and river nymph caught by him in the form of a fish from a stream. The kings of Sutnga extended their way over the plains. It was during the reign of U Parbat Ray in 1500 A.D. the Jaintia Kingdom was extended to the plains and established the capital at Jaintiapur, the principal seat of the Jaintia Kingdom.

U Parbat Ray reigned from 1500 to 1516 A.D. He was followed by Majha Gosain who reigned till 1532 A.D. Bura Parbat Ray rules from 1532 to 1548. After Burha Parbat Ray, Bar Gosain became the ruler. Bijay Manik succeed Bar Gosain in 1564. Pratap Ray followed Bijay Manik and Dhan Manik followed Pratap Ray. Dhan Manik was known to have been reigning at the close of the sixteenth century. After Dhan Manik, Jasa Manik (1605-1625), Sundar Ray (1625-1635), Chota Parbat Ray (1635-1669), Pratap Singh (1669) and Lakshmi Narayan (1669-1697) ruled the dynasty in successive years. Ram Singh I followed Lakshmi Narayan who reigned until 1708 A.D. He came into collision with the Kacharis and also with the Ahoms. Jay Narayan ruled from 1708 A.D. After Jay Narayan, Bar Gosain became the ruler. He enjoyed as usually long reign of nearly 40 years. There is a saying that Bar Gosain and his sister Gauri Kumari were taken captive by the syiem of Khairam, bur escaped by the aid of men send by Amar Singh, the syiem of Cherrapunji. Two villages in the Jaintia Parganaswere held rent-free by the Chief of the latter State, and it is said that they were given to Amar Singh as a reward for his services on this occasion.

Chatra Singh succeed Bar Gosain in 1770 and he was the first ruler of Jaintia to came into collision with the British. In 1734, the Jaintia State is said to have been conquered by the British force under Major Henniker, but it was restored on payment of fine. Jatra Narayan succeeded Chatra Singh in 1781 and was himself succeeded by Bijay Narayan in 1786. Ram Singh II succeeded by Rajendra Singh who was desposed in 1835 on the annexation of the country by the British.

The above Jaintia rulers were actually the masters of the plain areas of the Jaintia Parganas. In fact, the inhabitants of the Jaintia Hills were free from the purview of the above rulers. It may, perhaps, be concluded that the inhabitants of the Jaintia Hills had already formed a single State in 1500 A.D. and that year may be taken roughly as the date when they became the master of the Jaintia Parganas.

According to Gait (1925 : 259) the dominions of the Rajas of Jaintia included two entirely distinct tracts of country, namely, the Jaintia Hills which was inhabited by the Synteng, and the plains country, south of these hills and north of the Barak river, in the sylhet district, known as the Jaintia Parganas, inhabited by the Bengali Hindus and Muhammadans. The former tract was the original home of the dynasty. The latter tract was an annexation, but it was this area which was mentioned in Puranik and Tantrick literature as containing one of the fifty-one famous shrines sacred to Durga.

The Jaintia Rajas converted to Hinduism after they settled down in the plains. They were the devotees of the Sakti cult. Their involvement in human sacrifice might be the cause of the annexation of the Kingdom by the British in 1935.

III

The Jaintia Kings had relations with their neighboring Kingdoms, like the Ahoms, the Kacharis, the Koches and the Khyrim to the west. According to the Koch chronicles, both the Jaintias and the Khyrim kings were involved in wars with the Koches in the middle of the 16th century. The Jaintia King had lost his life in the war and his son was installed in his place as tutelary head.

Gait (1925 : 259) states that the Jaintias had an encounter with the Ahoms around 1707 A.D. during the reign of the Jaintia King Ram Singh I. The Ahom King Rudra Singha made an invasion of the Jaintia Kingdom. The people of the hills were not happy with Ram Singh because of the ill treatment made by the Jaintia Rajah with the Kachari King Tamradhvaj. The Kacari king managed to send a message to the Ahom king, Rudra Singha, who immediately wrote to Ram Singh demanding the release of the Kachari king. The Ahom king Rudra Singh's decision was not only to obtain submission of Ram Singh but also to annex the Jaintia Kingdom. However, alarmed the hill people and while they could not prevent the capture of their king who was taken away to offer personal obeisance to the Ahom king, they were determined to protect their independence. They took the assistance of the Khyrim chiefs and some 200 independent Khasi villages to repel the Ahoms. But they could not with stand the attacks of the Ahom forces, they held there own in the form of warfare that they were skillful in, that is, by restoring the guerrilla tactics. Thus, they managed to destroy many of the Ahom garrisons set up in the hills. The Ahoms inturn launched attacks on settled villages like Nartiang in the hills and on Jaintiapur which they destroyed, putting many of its inhabitants as prisoners. In the meantime, Ram Singh had made his submission to the

Ahom king who also demanded the surrender of the Jaintia nobles. Soon afterwards, Ram Singh died and was succeeded by his nephew, Rajendra Singh. The Ahom chronicles are silent about the aftermath and it may be assumed that peace between the Ahoms and the Jaintias was restored.

The most important history of the Jaintias was a skirmish that took place in 1774 between the British force and the Jaintias. There is no definite record, even from the British sources, as to the cause of this engagement, but probably it was due to some dispute over the boundary between the Jaintia Kingdom and the newly acquired British territory, involving the question of navigation rights in the river forming a natural boundary between the two. The engagement thus took place almost immediately after the British had obtained the Diwani of Bengal from the Mughals and succeeded to their authority over the far flung domains of the Mughals in the Province of Bengal. Moreover, the advent of the British into the region coincided with a period of decline in the history of the Jaintia Kingdom.

The establishment of the Jaintia rule over extensive tract in the plains, both north and south of the original kingdom, brought much affluence to the kings. It also led to progressive weaking of the traditional ties between the kings and their people in the hills. In the traditional ties between the kings and their people in the hills. In the traditional system, a distinction was always maintained between "natural" subjects and conquered subjects. Although both were termed as "Ki Khun" i.e., "children", there were always a difference between those called as "Ki Khun Ki Hajar" (means children thousands or rightful children) and "Ki Khun Kliar-Wait" (children won at the point of the sword).

IV

The Jaintia Kingdom continued till the coming of the British in the eighteenth century. The office of the king or *Syiem* was heredity, and succession was based on the matriliny principle, that is, one's sister's son will succeed to his mother's brother's office. In case, the *Syiem* lacks any relative, succession is decided by means of divination. Gassah (1989) reported that "the principle of divination was actually restored to in the case of U-Syiem Ram Singh II (1790-1832) with the help of local bird called *padia* or parrot giving the oracle".

The whole system would have continued had it not been for the impact of British Colonialism in the region. British administration had definately upset the system operating in Ri-Jaintia. Under the British, the first institution to go was that of kingship in 1835. After replacing the Rajah or the *Syiem*, the other rulers like the *Dolois* and others had to be under the British rule. Actually, the *Dolois* had then to bring their usual tributes of he goat to the British authorities at Cherrapunjee instead of taking them as usual to Jaintiapur.

The second institution to go was that of priesthood (*Langdoh*). The British had deprived the priest of his political role in presiding over the destiny of the Jaintia rulers. His role was then confined purely to religious matters. Whatever secular functions that had been enjoyed by the priest had been completely taken over by the British. The British authority could approve of the selection of *Doloi* and the *Doloi* was removed from the office in case of proved misbehaviour either to the people or to the British authorities. With the elimination of these two political institutions of the Jaintia Kingdom the democratic process that had existed in Ri-Jaintia in whatever dimension began to erode. The British authroties had become the absolute masters in Ri-Jaintia with no other authority to limit their power over the jaintias.

The only indigenous practices retained by the British were those of the institutions of a *Doloi*, a *Pator* and a *Waheb Chnong*. But even here the British had drastically reduced their traditional powers. The *Dolois* ceased to enjoy their traditional role of having a provincial governor of a *Raid* or *Illakas* and had practically became the commissioned agents of the British. This curtailment of their power was, however, only between them and the British. On the contrary, the *Dolois* had gained more control over their people with the backing of the British authorities.

The British utilised the services of the traditional leaders to help them in subjugating and ruling the not so easily lay abiding Jaintias of the hills with minimum effort and expenditure. The people then were loyal to the *Dolois* not because he was their traditional ruler but because of the fear of his new found authority bestowed by the British. By enjoying more powers over petty civil and criminal matters, as was observed in the new system introduced by the British, the *Dolois* had sometime misused their powers to keep the people under control. This was the position of the traditional rulers in Jaintia Kingdom till India's Independence.

While discussing the power structure of the Jaintia Kingdom, Gassah (1991 : 14) states that "the role of the original clans in the nomination of candidate or candidates for the political office, did not give the non original clans the chance to always elect the right person. The whole process was neither clumsy nor lack of proper thinking but intentionally institutionalized to keep the reign of power and authority in the State with the original clan. In such a situation, it was doubtful whether democracy had really existed in pre-colonial Jaintia State. Structurally the Jaintia State was regarded as democratic one but operationally the structure was more responsive than democratic".

V

The neighbouring tribal chiefs like the Karbis, the Lalungs were under the control of the Jaintia Kingdom. Lyall (1908 : 152) states that the Karbis or the Mikirs "were formerly subject of the Khasi chiefs of Jaintia and the eastern most States of the Khasi Hills, and that they migrated thence to the territory subject to the Ahom Kings. During their sojourn in Khasi – land they assimilated much; dress, ornaments, personal names, methods of divination, funeral ceremonies, memorial stones, all came from the Khasis" The author further says that the Karbi is a pratrilineal society and their social fabric is based upon clearly marked exogamous groups. They call their clans by the Jaiatia term *Kur*, but there is no trace of the matriarchal family as found among the Jaintias.

Since time immemorial the Karbis had been the subjects of the jaintias till Independence. There was a good deal of cultural exchange between these two communities yet the matriarchal system of the Jaintias, a pre-dominant characteristic of the people, did not find place in the social-cultural life of the Karbis.

The Karbis speak of the eastern portion of the Jaintia Hills bordering on the Kopili River as their original habitat. They call this region as Nihang which may perhaps be connected with Rongkhang or Ronghang (the traditional capital of the Karbi chief). Lyall (1908 : 3) also confirms it by saying that "they have dim traditions of a king of their own in the good olden days, whom they call *Sot Recho*. His seat is said to have been in Rongkhang (or Ronghang) perhaps connected with Jaintia".

It is clear that the Karbis were a part of the jainti monarchy and perhaps they had their traditional democratic system in line with their erstwhile master of the jaintias. The traditional Karbi democratic form of society combined with the Jaintia democratic formed the substratum of the pre-Independence political system in this part of the country.

Form the above discussion it can be said that the whole structure of the Jaintia Kingdom has its own growth. It appears to have its root in the soil itself The traditional power structure of the Jaintia Kingdom was in vogue since time immemorial when the whole of the Jaintia Hills was a virgin land, being untouched by sort of external forces. Hence, this elaborate system of Jaintia Kingdom is singularly significant of a democratic set up away from colonial variety. If for the sake of debate and deliberation it is held that the Jaintias had borrowed this system from others still the significance of the structure as bearing the fine democratic value is in no way diminished. In this case, the credit must be given to the Jaintias who have designed and formulated this system. It could, however, be admitted that the Jaintia brand of democracy is somewhat different from the real democracy where the original clans were given the right and privilages to hold the offices and run the administration in their own way.

REFERENCES

1. Bhuyan, S.K. 1937 *Jayantia Buranji* Gauhati Department of Historical & Antiquarian studies.
2. Gait, E.K. 1925 *History of Assam* Gauhati LBS Publication.

3. Gassah, L.S. 1989 Sequences in Development in Jaintia Hills. A Study of Tradition, Continuity and Change. In *Sequence of Development in North East India* New Delhi Omson Publication.
4. Gassah, L.S. 1991 Founding Clans, Their Role in Jaintia Traditional Polity Formation. *Journal of N.E.I.C.S.S.R.* 16:1:8-15.
5. Lyall, C. 1908 *The Mikirs* London David Nutt. (Reprinted United Publishers, Gauhati).
6. Pakem, B. 1977 The Changing Power Structure of the Political Chief trainship. *Journal of of N.E.I.C.S.S.R.* 1:1:13.
7. Simon, I.M. 1995 *Gazetteer of India Jaintia Hills District.* Shillong Art and Culture Department Govt. of Meghalaya.

12

NARRATIVE, RITUAL AND HISTROCIAL EVENTS : THE JAINTIA IDENTITY

Soumen Sen

In recent years identity question has been perceived as a major issue in social science research. To serve the purpose of defining a smaller group of people in a larger system, often perceived as an indigenous group in the current global debate, the term ethnicity has been introduced. The developments over the post-world war decades have seen the upsurges of social, political and autonomy movements with the assertion of rights by these minority groups. The debate persists, not always achieving a consensus, but, somehow researchers have been successful in identifying a few attributes. These attributes are mostly on the cultural contents of a group's would view. However, the intensity of a consciousness of a distinct identity may also be regulated by other forces including political developments, historical events and geographical mobility.

Cultural identity is related to ethnicity, a term derived from the word 'ethnos' of Greek origin. This polysemantic word, *ethnos*, means people and may be used in a broad sense as well as in a restricted sense. Communities with very large or very small populations, and again both archaic and modern people alike may be called ethnos. In a restricted sense we may identity an ethnos, for instance, the Jaintia ethnos, by taking out from the entire mankind a distinct group of people who call themselves Jaintia and all of whom share certain features in common which in their entirely are not present in any other group an ethnos in such a restricted sense is called *ethnicos*[1]. A particular ethnicos possesses certain common attributes that include folklore, which is related to ethnic consciousness. One element has however, been recognised as most significant i.e. awakening as the foremost experience of ethnic identity. This awakening, or the consciousness of a group's potential for a foothold for self-ascertain is linked with the identification of a cultural universe traced in the ethnic tradition. The group looks back and finds the essentials for a solidarity movement to achieve its perceived legitimate place. Some of these essentials are the cultural symbols of expressions found in the distinct world view.

One of the most significantly defining features of the world view of an ethnicos is to cosmogony and its perception of the universe. The *genre* of folklore that carries such perception is known as myth. Myths, particularly the origin myths, express the identity and status aspirations of an ethnicos and reflect its world-view and religion-social ethos, which is perpetual. They are oral narratives, usually taken as sacred, telling of divine beings and semi-divine heroes, the origin of the earth, the world, the people, through the desires and acts of the divine beings and serve as collective cosensus on shared norms and values emphasizing societal solidarity. Ritual events through mythic performances strengthens this solidarity at the cognitive level by enhancing a realm of values, beliefs as well as actions in the structures of the society. Ethnic identity is recurrently emphasized to achieve both structural and functional cohension through both ritual and mythic performances.

Needless to say that myths, the oral narratives, originated at a time when man had no valid answers to many or vexed questions of existence. The people then attempted answers, necessarily positive and graphic, conferring powers on god, various deities and semi-divine heroes credited with creation and care. One important issue is the social system and customs that the people would want to survive and continue. There is thus an attempt to relate the mythological system with the kinship system. The stories are told again and again, particularly in the annual festival and ritual event. Thus gain authority through such repetition of episodes and faith gets strengthened. Describing the creation of the universe, the origin and placement of the ethnicos is a very important strategy of such narratives. Both theological and social concerns get combined.

THE KHASI-JAINTIA IDENTITY AND ORAL NARRATIVES

For many years, the peoples inhabiting the Khasi and Jaintia Hills of Meghalaya were broadly called the Khasis. This generic name was in vogue and these peoples were divided and identified in five sub-groups: the *Khynriam* of the central plateau, the *pnar* or *synteng* or *Jaintia* of the Jaintia Hills, *War* of the northern region, *Bhoi* in the north and *Lyngam* of the Western border. But recently an opinion has been generated to establish that the Jaintias have a separate and distinct identity and are divided into six sub-groups: the *Bhoi*, the *Biata*, the *Hadem*, the *Lalung*, the *Pnar* and the *War*[2].

However, some scholars have maintained that 'there are many proofs in support of the argument that the Khasis and Pnars are descended from the same ancesters' (Simon 1966 : 49). This argument is based on oral traditions and a narrative has been quoted:

In the beginning there was only one woman in the Talang clan named Iawtalang. She had nine daughters who were all very industrious. So devoted were they to their work that even when the youngest was on the point of child bearing, the eight elder sisters left her at home with her husband, a man of the Dkhar clan. The youngest sister's husband was so furious that he cooked the after-birth and gave it to the elder sisters on their refura, saying that it was the meat of a sacrificial cook. After they had finished eating he taunted them saying that they were devourers their own kith and kin. In intense shame they fled the village and almost all of them founded other clans in other localities. One of them went to Chyrmang village, retaining however her original clan name another went to thangbuli and founded the buam clan. 'Buam' originated from two words, 'bu-a' (eat) and 'am' (Water), which she uttered when she learned what she had eaten : "Lah Kaba bua am" (Better to have eaten plain water). Another went towards Rymbai, but because she stayed a night at Myntdu, the clan she founded is known as Nongtdu. Another went to Sohmynting where she founded the Pyrtuh clan after the religious celebration called the Pyrtuh. Another went to Khasi Hills and there she founded the syntung clan; another founded the Suting clan. Some people say that both these clans are one and the same. Another went to Maroblang and founded the Talang clan and yet another went to Nongtarlang and her progeny being the first to arrive in the locality became the Lyngdohs or priest clan. The last one, Ka Nialang by name, remained alone at Pamchadong and there she founded the clan known to this day by her name (Simon 1966 : 49-50).

Whether the progany of 'the seven huts' of the mythic narrative of '*ki Hynniew Trep*' include the Jaintias cannot be said for sure since the generic term Khasi is mentioned only. But the versions from both the Khasi and Jaintia Hills narrate the same myth of origin. The most widely spread version mention of a place of habitation of *Ki Hynniew Trep* called Sophetbneng, a hill top in Khasi Hills. In one version, God initially created sixteen families who stayed with him in heaven and could commute between heaven and earth by means of a ladder in the shape of a tree on a hill top known as *Sohpetbneng*. Later seven of these families (*Ki Hynniew Trep*) expressed their desire to remain on earth. God granted them their wish but remarked the ladder[3]. In another version, in the golden age after creation, Man had personal relation with God and could commute between heaven and earth but in course of time *Ki Hynniew Trep* the ancestors of the Khasi race, drifted away from God to choose their own way and thus the golden bridge (the tree at sohpetbneng) collapsed but communication was restored later. It happened when a tall big tree on the top of U Diengiei peak overcasting the earth with darkness (signifying man's spiritual crisis) with its overspreading branches and leaves, was ultimately felled down by God[4]. In yet another version, on one day when only seven women were on earth an evil spirit cut off the tree which served as the ladder for communication between earth and heaven and these seven women were forced to remain on earth and their progeny came to be known as *Ki Hynniew Trep* settled on earth they were given three commandments by God which form the essence of Khasi religion, *Ka Niam Khasi*.

There are some new elements in a version of the narrative collected from Jaintia Hills (Source : Christobin Rymbai, R.T. Rymbai and O.P. Lytan of Jowai, Jaintia Hills)[7]. The new elements are: the presence of Syiem U Lakriah, the sem-divine hero through whom the people received the commandments from God: the presence of a supreme golden, *Ka Blei Synshar* and of the mother earth, *Ka Blei Rimman.* The narrative is as follows :

There were sixteen families in heaven. Of whom seven were sent to earth. They could visit heaven by a golden ladder. The nine families living with God in heaven could also visit the earth by that ladder. The seven families on earth were led by Syiem U Lakriah. Her and the members of the seven families had divine qualities for which other creatures on earth accepted their leadership. Order was restored. But the seven families soon found that the world was full of stones. There was no soil and they faced difficulties in cultivating. U Lakriah, therefore, went to heaven to ask for soil from God. God directed the supreme goddess, Ka Blei Synshar, to give U Lakriah three basketful of earth (soil) from heaven. U Lakriah came back with these baskets and covered the stones with soil. (In another version, *Ka Blei Synshar* sent *ka Blei Rimmans*, the mother earth, to cover the stones with soil. It is also said that God could only be approached through *Blei Rimmand* by libations). When evil spirits made life miserable, people prayed to God and solicited his presence. God came to earth, met U Lakriah in some unknown place and conveyed his wishes and advice. These were known as *Niam* on commandments. God also decreed that He could be approached by prayer, libation and sacrifice. U Lakriah would ascertain the wishes of God by divination.

In all these narratives, one element is common i.e. the seven families and the Khasis (and perhaps including the Jaintias) are the progany of these seven families and are known as the children of *Ki Hynniew Trep.* The mythic narrative of *Ki Hynniew Trep* is repeatedly referred to enhance the identity consciousness: 'The Khasi-Pnars, to this day, in times of storm and stream, of stir and strife, whenever there is a call for the unity of the tribe, invoke the name of *Ka Hynniew Trep* (rymbai 1998: 166).

MYTH, RITUAL AND IDENTITY

The *Behdienkhlam* festival-cum-ritual held annually at Jowai in Jaintia Hills I associated with an identity consciousness. During the colonial days, the British administration forced the stoppage of the performance of this festival. It was, however, revived after the independence of India at the initiative of an association of the *Jaintias*, called Seinraj, with its headquarters at Jowai and branches in Shillong and other places. This association was formed to fight for the religious and cultural rights of the Jaintias' (H. Rymbai 1979 : 185).

Although the *Behdienkhlam* festival is a harvest festival organized after the sowing of seeds and rites are performed to drive away the evil spirits of plague and pestilence to ensure good harvest, some rites are also eventually directed towards the veneration of the ancestors. The effectiveness of the rituals performed is rooted in the emotions, both social and religious, along with the narration of two myths : those of *Syiem U Lakriah* and *Saw kpho. Rites* are performed to drive away all evils that plague the human life – *behdien* means driving away with sticks and *Khlam* means plague or peslilence. *Khlam* is also described as shedemon causing epidemic, *dien* (or *dieng*) means tree. Rites are performed in different phases in one month preceding the final three-day festival. During the month, members of different clans would clean their clan-cematery. They would bring tree-trunks from forests and place them in a common place on the first day of the last three days to be taken to respective localities on the last day. A particular tree-trunk called *khnong* would be taken to a locality, Shilliangraj. In the early morning it would be mutually planted at a place in that locality. The chief (*daloi*), other officials and large number of people would then assembled at the courtyard of the house of the chief priests (*Lyngdoh*) where the daloi would consecrate the narrator (*parom*) by pouring rice-beer on the courtyard who would narrate the myths of *U Lakhriah* and *Saw kpoh.* The myth of U Lakriah (already quoted) narrates how the race originated from seven families and their leader Syiem U Lakriah got the three Commandments of *Ka Niam* from God. The myth of *Saw kpoh*, however, tells how the clans that settled and around Jowai originated from four (*saw*) wombs (*kpoh*). The narrative is as follows :

Once upon a time four wandering sisters, Ka Bon, Ka tein, Ka Wet and ka Doh, along with their menfolk, arrived at a spot near Jowai in Jaintia Hills. There was a big stone nearby. The sisters decided to stay there overnight. At the end of the night, Ka Bon heard a sound, woke up and saw the stone dancing. She was horrified, called everyone, and was about to flee when the stone stopped dancing and said, 'Oh, children of God, do not run away, stay with us here. I assure you that no harm will come to you, Myself and my brothers shall guard you from all evils and we shall walk the four corners. Our maid servant the river Ka Myntdu will save you faithfully'. The name of the stone-spirit was U Mukhai. He and his brother, U Mushiang, U Muralong and U Mulong, guard the four corners of Jowai where the progeny of the four sisters live. From the *saw kpoh* (the four wombs) or clans come the religious and secular chiefs, *Lyngdoh*, *daloi*, *parton* and *basan.* Rites are performed every year to venerate the four sisters with the chanting of this myth. The stone deities who guard the four corners or gates are also venerated with sacrifices[8].

Dramatization of myths in ritual context is wel known. Such dramatization through symbolic performances in the rites following the chanting of narratives reinforces a consciousness that is considered most essential in social context. Ritual performances for reinforcing faith in mythic narratives involve not only the narrator and performer but the community at large. Enactment draws upon traition linking past events, mythical or otherwise, with the present, and sats a course for the future. Performance in the sense in doing again in a legitimating way.

Ritual events with narratives play the most strategic roles in enhancing a realm of values, beliefs as well as actions, in the structures of the society. Identity is recurrently emphasized to achieve both structural and functional cohension through these performances. In *Behdienkhlam*, in its ritual events and narratives, the Jaintia identity is re-inforced annually.

THE HISTORICAL EVENT

The issue of a separate identity of the Jaintias perhaps got strengthened by a historical event of a political formation, the Jaintia kingdom, around thirteenth century A.D. The situation prevailing in the Hills and the political administrative arrangements made before the establishment of the kingdom to ensure a sense of unity among the Jaintias has been narrated by Pakem in these words, 'With the increase in population and size of the territory (*Raids* or *Elakas*) consisting of a group of villages, secular functions increased. This necessitated the bifurcation of sacred and secular functions. While the sacred function was retained by the *Lyngdoh*, that of secular function was then entrusted to an official called *U Daloi.* Again when the number of daloiships increased there was a feeling among the Jaintias to establish unity among themselves. This gave way to the growth of the institution of the kingship in Jaintia Hills. To make it more acceptable to the people, the office of kingship was originally occupied by a person who was supposed to be divinely ordained through a miraculous birth of the royal family out of a mermaid *Ka Li Dakha.* Since this incident was supposed to have occurred within Sutnga daloiship, the royal dynasty was then called *Ki Syiem Sutnga* (the Sutnga dynasty). It was this dynasty which had brought all the political units of Jaintia Hills under one central authority with wider latitude of powers to the units called *Raid* or *Elakas*. With the conquest of the Jaintia plains in the thirteenth century A.D. the central authority had, for the first time, its own territory where its writs covered every aspect of administration.' (Pakem 1990 : 80-81).

This is how, though historical process, a Jaintia identity was perhaps generated. Oral narrative were referred to establish the Jaintia hegemony. It is known that the Jaintias have another name, *Pnar*, which is perhaps their *endoethnonym*, i.e. the name given to themselves by an ethnicos for self-identification Jaintia does not seem to be an *endoethnonym*[9]. This has perhaps been derived from the name of the Jaintia kingdom. But how did the kingdom get its name?

There are a number of explanations one view among the earlier historian was that the kingdom got its name from Jaintiapur, its capital, located in Jainita Parganas in the plains part of the kingdom. This explanation was based on the *Puranic* and *Tantric* texts which suggest that the kingdom got its name from *Jayanti Devi* or *Jainteswari*, an incarnation of Goddess Durga or Gouri, the reigning deity of the kingdom with her shrine at Jaintiapur. There is also a Hindu myth in justification of this information. Since the kingdom got its name from Jaintia Parganas or Jaintiapur or from Jayanti Devi, the reigning dirty of the kingdom as the myth suggests, and from whom desconded the royal family[10], the hills with many a small divisions with local chiefs, got a new name, Jaintia. The people inhabiting the hills also got a new name, Jaintia, an *exoethnonym* i.e. a name given to them by outsiders. In course of time, however, it became an *endoethnonym* as well, by acceptance.

There is another explanation, a linguistic explanation that the name Jaintia might have been derived from *Synteng*, another racial name (perhaps an *exohethnonym*) of the people who now call themselves Jaintia. This explanation is also based on a fact that the historically known lines of kings of Jaintiapur were known as *Syntengs*[11].

There is yet another argument that the word Jaintia has been derived from *Sutug*, a place name. It is believed, through oral tradition, that the Jaintia kingdom was established by the chief (*Daloi*) of a pre-state polity in Jaintia Hills, called Sutuga. Historical evidences also suggest that the kings of Jaintiapur came from the Hills and they belonged to the Pnar or Synteng community. Oral narratives particularly that of *Ka hih Dakha* and *U Loh Ryndi* also seem to justify this claim[13].

Thus, whether genetically, linguistically or culturally, the Jaintias are distinguished as or separate ethnic group and not a sub-group of the people given a generic name, it is certain that over a historical period they started claiming for an identity. The claim sought support from narrative, ritual and historical events.

NOTES

1. For a detailed discussion, see S.K. Acharaya, 1990.
2. See Pakem 1990, Majumdar 1981 and Das 1978.
3. See R.T. Rymbai 1979; 110.
4. See Mawrie 1981 ; 5-6.
5. See Simon 1966 ; 29.
6. For details see R.T. Rymbai 1979 ; 111-12.
7. Seen Sen 1985 ; 168-69.
8. Source : Cristobin Rymbai, R.T. Rymbai and O.P. Lytan of Jowai, See Sen 1985 ; 170.
9. For detail discussion see Sen 1998 ; 85-91.
10. See Sen 1985 ; 201-04.
11. For a detailed discussion see, Chatterji, 1951:167.
12. See Pakem, 1990: 81-81.
13. See Sen 1985 : 197-201.

REFERENCES

1. Acharya, S.K. (1990) 'Ethnic, Processes in North-Eastern India' (in) B.Pakem.Ed. *Nationality, Ethnicity and Cultural Identity in North East India*. New Delhi : Omsons, pp. 69-108.
2. Chatterji, S.K. (1951) *Kirata-Jana-Krti*, Calcutta : The Asiatic Society.
3. Das, B.M. (1978) *Variations in Physical Characteristics in the Khasi Population of North-East India*, Gauhati : Dattta Barma & Co.
4. Majumdar, D.N. (1981) 'Forward' to *A Tribe in Transition : The jaintias of Meghalaya*. H.L. Deb Roy, New Delhi : Cosmo.
5. Mawrie, H. Anderson (1981) *The Essence of the Khasi Religion*. Shillong : Seng Khasi.
6. Pale, B. (1990) 'Social and Political Institutions of the Jaintias of Meghalaya' (in) Jayanta Sarkar and B. Datta Ray. Eds. *Social and Political Institutions of the Hill People of North-East India*, Calcutta : Anthropological Survey of India, pp. 80-92.
7. Rymbai, H. (1979) 'The Birth of Seim Raj' (in) U Hipshon Roy. Ed. *The Khasi Heritage*. Shillong : Seng Khasi pp. 185-86.
8. Rymbai, R.T. (1979) 'Some Aspects of the Religion of the Khasi-Pnar' (in) U Hipshon Roy. Ed. *The Khasi Heritage*. Shillong : Seng Khasi. pp. 110-18.
9. ________ (1993) 'Christian Missions and the Indigenous Religion of the Khasi-Pnar' (in) Souman Sen Ed. *Religion in North-East India*. New Delhi : New Delhi : Uppal Publishing House. Pp. 68-102.
10. Sen, Soumen (1985) *Social and State Formation in Khasi – Jaintia Hills : A Study of Folklore*. New Delhi : B.R. Publishing Corporation.
11. __________(1998) 'Endoethnonym and Exoethnonym of, and Ethnicos : Identity and Folklore *South Indian Folklorist*. Vol. 2 pp. 85-91.
12. Simon, I.M. (1966) *Khasi and Jaintia Tales and Beliefs* Gauhati : Gauhati University.

13

IDEOLOGICAL INFLUENCES ON THE JAINTIA RULLING FAMILY

Shobhan N Lamare

The term Jaintia is used to denote a group of people mainly inhabiting Jaintia Hills district of Meghalaya(1).The Jaintias can also be found in the neighbouring hill district of Khasi hills (Meghalaya), Karbi Anglong, North Cachar hills, in the plains of Cachar of Assam and also in the adjoining-district of Sylhet in Bangladesh(2),The total area of the Jaintia Hills as estimated in 1868 was 2,100 Sq.miles(3). Orginally the Jaintia kingdom consisted of three parts viz;the Jaintia hills,neighbouring plains in Sylhet and territories in present day Nowgong district.The hilly portion was the orginal home of the rulling family(4).

In the l8th century the kingdom was bounded in the north by Gobha-Sonapur, south by the river Surma, east by the river Kupli and in the west by the Brahmaputra.At times some principalities of Kamrup and Karimganj were included in this kingdom.The hilly portion was peopled by the Jaintias,the Jaintia plains of Sylhet by the Bengali and the Nowgong portion by the Jaintias, Dimasas, Lalungs and other tribes(5). The rulling family belonged to the Jaintia tribe-Pnar(6) and were considered to be the first settlers in this region and are the off-shoot of the mon-khmer race of South-East Asia and had ascended the hills through the Assam valley(7) where the exact date cannot be visualised but falls back to antiquity.

The pnars for centuries had long contacts with the people of the plains particularly that of the Surma valley and this had a significant impact on their political, economic and social life. The plain areas of the Syiem of Jaintia were inhabited pre-dominantly by the Bengali Hindus and muslims whose main occupation was agriculture.These people had taken to extensive agricultural works where most of the jungle land was brought under cultivation.It was again during this time that Hinduism started to make in roads into the Jaintia kingdom.Hinduism standing as an organised religion,having clearly defined doctrines and a large number of followers attracted the attention of the .Raja and his followers and mere soon converted to Hinduism.They formed a distinct community in the capital of the kingdom(8).Along side with this Brahmanical doctrines have made such progress,where most of the leading men in the kingdom have adopted them including the spiritual instructors(9).

In the hills, Nartiang which was the summer capital of the king was the principal centre of Hinduism and Hindu temples attributed to goddess Kali and Shiv was constructed and is still in use till this day. On the other hand in Jaintiapur which was again the winter capital the goddess Kali was worshipped along with their tribal counterparts. These deities were given local honorifics, like the Hindu god of artisan Biswakarma was called U Biskurom; Siva as U Mahadev Khlow; Lakshmi as Lakhi; Durga as Parvati; Chandi as ka Ron Chandi.

The muslim inhabitants of the plains had their own share of influence and this can be seen in the festival of the people where they adopted the construction of Rakhs locally known as Rots during the Behdienkhlam festival. Alonp with these, effigies of a huge man is made which is carried along while dancing and which was to be destroyed later. This idea of making effigies representing a huge man or giants is still complex and difficult to ascertain as to whether it was indigeneous or was borrowed from other religions. As Brahmanism gained ground,the tantric cult also found its way into the Pnar life and Human sacrifices were carried out in the hills especially during the Durga pujas(10).These type of assimilation which had been going on for generations together had often baffled a careless onlooker as to the religion of the people.Though some of the Jaintias had taken to Hinduism, the majority of the people are still the ardent followers of the indegeneous religion called Niam-Tre. Infact the Hindu converts form just a small section of the community.

Some reserchers and historians prefered to call the religion of the people as primitive Hinduism and therefore considered it to be rustic, superstitious and unsophisticated. This again can be attributed to the parochial attitude of the people when it was found out that some sanskritic elements were learned and then reformed by the villagers to become a part of their local cult.These type of duality gained more importance when the Raja and his people accepted Hinduism as their religion and thinking themselves to be more superior than the others and that their folk tradition were primitive and backward. This had led to a crisis at an earlier stage where the people do not have a proper explanation to this type of development. In fact a search for standardisation to eradicate the same is being carried out from those early stages.

The Jaintia people living in the plains, mostly in the southern part made them to limitate the Caste system of those people in the plains.However, such imitations did not make a pure form of the caste system as it existed in the plains. It is true that certain clans were entrusted with certain specific functions, those clans were not differentiated from the rest of the population.At most the system was half way between the caste system and the class system(11). This conclusion on the other hand cannot be drawn in the same parrallel with the Pnar people of the hills.In certain areas it might appear that there was some kind of an influence where we find references to Ki Kmai Kur who had access to political rights and Ki Khian Kur who does not have this right and are considered as immigrants(12).

Another area of influence can be seen when the king would hold durbar. Here ministers, senapati and other leading officers would sit on the three sides of the king,but according to priority.The royal umbrella bearer,and the bearer of hookah would remain standing and serve the king from time to time.The king was addressed as Bapthakur while his sister was addressed as Thakurmai and her husband as Kuwar(13).The royal court was always adorned by a galaxy of scholars most of whom were Brahmins.The Raj pundits or royal priests held an im portant position in the state.The Rajas gifted land to the Brahmins.They established temples and were assigned lands for their maintenance(14). They also patronised learning(15). The coins and inscriptions were issued in Sanskrit language but in Bengali script and contain Hindu legends. The official records and diplomatic correspondence were maintain in Bengali.

In the social life of the people differences manifested itself in the living pattern particularly in the plains. The well-to-do people used to put on Muga-dhoti and Paguree.The poorer people used cotton clothes.The priviledge group used bamboo umbrellas with handles,the similar umbrellas used by the poorer sections were without handles.The common people were not generally allowed to use umbrella and gold ornaments.They had to obtain special permission from the Raja for the use of these items on payment of a fee. Permission was also required for making stone staircase of a house (16).

The political institution of the Jaintias was also not free from these type of influence. The Hindu system had slowly permeated into the traditional system of managing the state. It was with this that a crack in the democratic nature of the Jaintia state started to become evident and an era of erosion of democracy had begun. The experience of the Rajas autocratic rule in the plains made the Dalois or the chiefs in the hills to immitate the Raja's style of functioning. The Dalois then regarded their Raids on the same level with that of the zamindar in the plains, where a transition was inevitable. It was from this time onwards that the popular democratic rulers of the hills turned into petty oligarchs. It will not be out of context to state here that by the time the British came and started to influence the Jaintia political scene, Jaintia democracy had turned out to be merely an oligarchy.

Interestingly, prior to these type of developments, the exposure to Brahmin myths and legends had another important impact on the status of the ruling tribal clan. The concept like the 'divine origin' of kings found its way into the Pnar society. This gave a strong impetus in strengthning the institution of kingship where the myths like the miraculous birth of the royal family out of a mermaid ka Li Dakha was projected. This type of myths fostered the cognate clans, the bordering tribes including the technologically more advanced Bengalis to integrate and in the process ensured the domination of the Brahmins in the affairs of the state: This to a very great extent helped the Raja to consolidate his rule and culturally influenced all the subjects including the people of the hills. The reasons as to why the Pnars do not take beef during those years can also be said to be the influence of Hinduism from the plains. During the time of festivals and merry making cultural influences are evident where apart from the dress pattern (which had been mentioned earlier), musical instruments from the plains like the tabla, harmonium would supplement the traditional Jaintia instruments.

Another area where the effect is very pronounced can be seen in the day to day life of the people. Here we find that in the field of agriculture, the better methods of cultivation of the field like the using of the plough and bullocks were borrowed over the plains. In the construction of houses the people use to smear the front of their houses with red earth and cowdung. Influences can also be seen in their food culture and the names given to the people particularly with the Rajas where Hindu names became more fashionable, but the change was gradual. There was also the borrowing of words, where along with the Pnar dialect, the Bengali words are being used and interpreted according to the convenience of the people with a slight modification here and there.

These developments accompanied by a close interaction with the people of the plains made the Jaintia society to adapt and adjust to the process of change. These again were taken and modified accordingly to serve their own purpose. However, the Pnar society did not make a break from their traditional culture and the assimilation did not wane out their age old practices like matriliny, religion, marriage and others. This was made possible because of the realisation that the degree of its survival depended much on its own cultural self image and identity which were enshrined in the oral tradition of the people.

REFERENCES

1. S.N.Lamare, The Cultural Transition of The Pnars from The Middle of The l9th Century To The First Half of The 20th Century (unpublished M.phil Dissertation) p.1
2. B.Pakem, Social and Political Institution of the Jaintiae of Meghalaya" in Jayanta. Sarkar and B.Dutta Ray, Social and Political Institutions of the Hill People of North East India p.80
3. P.N.Dutta, Impact of the Vest on Khasi and Jaintia p.1
4. S.M.Ali, History of Jaintias p.1
5. J,B,Bhattacharjee, "Brahmanical Myths,Royal Legitimation and the Jaintia State Formation" in N.E.H.U. Journal of Social Sciences and Humanities.Vol.3; No.l, p.47; also in J.B.Bhattacharjee, Social and Polity. Formation in Pre-Colonial North Fast India, p.79; also see S.M.

Ali, op.cit pp.4 and 5; and also in R.M. Lahiri, The Annexation of Assam,pp· 151-157.

6. J.B.Bhattacharjee, op.cit
7. Ibid
8. S.M.Ali,op.cit p.72.
9. P.N. Dutta, op.cit p.9.
10. P.R.T. Gurdon, The Khasis, pp. 101-104; Edward Gait, Journal of the Asiatic Society of Bengal, Vol.,1898; and also in H.L.Debroy, A Tribe In Transition: The Jaintias of Meghalaya p.141
11. B.Pakem, op.cit p.88
12. J.B.Bhattacharjee, op.cit p.48
13. S.M.AIi, op.cit, p.70
14. J.B. Bhattacharjee, op.cit p.48
15. Raja Rajendra Sing was a devotee of Vaishnava.He was very fond of Jhulon songs and Hari Sankirtan and had himself composed some songs which are known to this.day. For details see S.M. Ali, op.cit p.60 and J.B.Bhattacharjee, op.cit p.53
16. J.B.Rhattacharjee op.cit

14

KHASI JAINTIA WOMEN: ROLE IN DECISION MAKING BODIES SOME OBSERVATIONS

Biloris Lyndem

The Khasis and Jaintias belong to the same stock. Ethnologists trace a relationship existing between them and a certain group of people from South East Asia. The Chief representative being the Mons or Talangs of Burma and the Khmer of Cambodia. Their nearest kinsmen are said to be the Palungs inhabiting the Shan states to the North East of Mandalay. As stated Meghalaya is the only state in the entire North east which follow matrilineal system drawing the lineage and takes the identity solely from the mother. The women here are very lucky because they are treated eqully with their male counterparts, but the head of the family is always the father. In this society the question of illigitimate child, child abandoning dowry and bride burning are unknown. Offsprings whether male or female are treated alike. On the whole the society is unique women are property holders and keeper of the family purse and other movable and immovable properties.

In a matrilineal society marriage is strictly exogamous i.e. outside the clan (Kur). There cannot be a greater sin than a coition between members of the Kurs '.

Women in Khasi & Jaintia society accorded high respect. At home women take care of the nursing and rearing of the children, supervision of the domestic activities, attending to the sick aged parents and other relatives in distress. This is the duty of the youngest daughter in both Khasi and Jaintia family. Khasi Jaintia women are very sociable. This is reflected in the structural pattern of their socio-political system, which by itself formed a social organisation from the family unit to the Hima or state. There is no caste or class system women are free to participate in any social activities.

The Khasi and Jaintia women are known to be hardworking, they contribute in many respect to the family income, by engaging themselves in different economic activities. They lend a helping hand in agriculture trade business or any activity. It is seen that they give a helping hand to their menfolk in many ways, collecting firewood weeding and harvesting. With the spread of education women home taken jobs in Government offices, many of them are working as doctors, engineers , college and university teachers and other profession and they are known for their dedication sincererity and efficiency. Both Khasi and Jaintia women have also shown their proficiency in trade and business. Another remarkable strength of the social structure is that there is a balance or a synthesis between the authority enjoyed by the maternal uncle, father and the mother. In its positive glory the social system endeavoured to bring out the best among the three units of authority by clearly defining their roles.

One unique feature of the society is that the man has a dual crown, being an uncle in his sister's house, and a father to his children. In his wife's house he is a father who is capable and able to support the family. He acts as a philosopher, a guide and a friend on all clan matter. The inheritance of the ancestral property for both Khasi and Jaintia goes to the youngest daughter (Khadduh) in the family. The youngest daughter cannot dispose the ancestral property without the consent of the male members. According the Gurdon the practice of matriarchal and the fact that the ancestral property is vested with the mother could be a mistake to suppose that the father is nobody in the Khasi and Jaintia family. The father has a strong position both in his wife's house as well in his mother's house.

Though women enjoyed a higher distinct status but yet restrictions were enforced especially in political affairs. Traditionally women did not have any place or role in decision making forum. Women were not allowed to attend any durbar or council. They were not given to speak or attend any meeting which concerned the political affairs. It is considered that deliberations decision, planning, and administration and policies and the burdens of management belong to men. This is an issue which raises a lot of questions, where women of Meghalaya are not given an opportunity in decision making bodies or they are shy to take part in political affairs? This need to be studied.

Coming to the crucial debate about women's defacto position in a matrilineal system (such as one that exists in the Khasi and Jaintia Hills) and to attempt to respond to the question whether the matrilineal system here offers a full and total empowerment to its women - it is important to examine the actual workings and the real position of Khasi Jaintia women in all ages, and in every sphere through the varied stages of matriliny as it existed in the past as it exists today and the final shape it should assume.

The Khasi and Jaintia Hills have for long remained a bastion and oasis of matriliny expanse of neighbouring patriarchal societies. The Khasi and Jaintia women has never been under the shadow of men as she has long been custodian of her family name (lineage) and property. However, the immense privileges quaranteed to her in other spheres is denied to her in matters or polity and public life. This has been an issue that has raised a few questions, for it represents a break with the past. A brief glimpse at history reveals that both the Khasi and Jaintias were quite comfortable with the woman as a ruler and an administrator. The fame of Ka Latympang and Ka Pring Sariang the queens of the Jaintia is well known. Despite many obstacles and difficulties Miss. Mavis Dunn Lyngdoh got elected as early as in 1937 similarly Mrs. Bonniely Khongmen became Member of Parliament in 1952 and now we have Mrs. Roshan Warjri, and Mrs. Maysalin War as an MLA. Mrs. Maya Rani Kyndiah a Jaintia women contested the election several times but not elected, she is still an active politician. The fore runners now are Phidalia Toi, Probity Nongpluh, social activists and others have come out with their agenda to get the support of other women. Prominent entrepreneurs are Mrs. Dolly Khonglah ,Mrs. M.J. Passah, Mrs. Edwina Lyngdoh, Mrs. Obilet Tariang and many more are coming up as successful business women.

As discussed earlier, despite the immense rights and privileges conferred by the matrilineal society, unwillingly, the traditional laws deprived the Khasi Jaintia women fundamental, political and human rights in the context of today's democratic liberal and modern society. The male exclusiveness in the Khasi Durbar is unconditionally excepted so also its arbitration in community matters. Women have no voice in the durbar even if they are allowed to attend, they cannot question the authority of the durbar and its decision.

As such this thinking becomes the accepted norm in the larger political sphere as well. Hence, the political parties are prone to mirror the attitudes of these traditional bodies. In the light of this, democracy becomes at best superficial and limited, in this atmosphere where women are debarred from all these all important constitutions, which decides and determine community rules. While legislation like the women's Reservation Bill what is urgently needed is a complete overhaul of the present patriarchal system and values which dominate the functioning the traditional society. The modern educated Khasi Jaintia women cannot accept any concept of democracy which excludes any one section of society. The Women's Reservation Bill and similar lagislations represent at best a temporary machanism, the real change has to start through effecting changes within the traditional system itself. As Panchayati Raj does not exists in the Khasi Jaintia Hills hence the revolutionary changes brought by the 73rd Ammendment leaves the woman here untouched.

As majority of political leaders in Meghalaya are men, they have made it clear that women in Meghalaya do not need reservation of seats in the Assembly as they are vested with enough power under matrilineal system. It is also felt that women legislators in the state also are against reservation. In their opinion women are better off than their counterparts elsewhere because of the matrilineal system. With all these women are not sitting idle they have made their voices to be heard in several platforms. Recently Probity Nongpluh a social activists won a case in the Guwahati High Court seeking one-third reservation for women in the Municipal poll. The matter is still hanging in the Supreme Court.

In Meghalaya all decision bodies are male dominated, where all the major decision are in the hands of men. Ther,efore, real improvement can only happen when the patriarchal mindset of these bodies is reversed.` It is only the inclusion of women in decision making process which will enable a change in attitudes in a far more effective manner than any legislation and ammendments. Further, the feminist agenda and female perspective on issues like family welfare, health population and literacy will be paid greater attention. What is needed now is to review the inherent and in-built the patriarchal component in the system. The society will move forward if there is an equal patnership between men and women.

REFERENCES

1. Bareh, Hamlet, 1967 p.15-17, The History and Culture of the Khasi People.
2. Chattopadhaya S.K., 1988 5-6, The Jaintias Cosmo Publication, New Delhi.
3. Singh K.S., Profile of India, Anthropoligical Survey of India, Segul Books Cal -1994 p 69.76
4. Gurdon PR.T., The Khasi Cosmo Publications, Delhi : 1975, p.82
5. Barkataki.S., Tribes of Assam, National Book Trust, India, New Delhi - 1969 p.42-43
6. Khasi Heritage, A collection of Essavs on Khasi Religion and Culture - Ri-Khasi Press, 1979.

15

MECHANISED FARMING FOR SLOPE LAND ORCHARDS IN JAINTIA HILLS

Susmita Priyadarshini

In Jaintia hills upland areas have been cultivated since the ancient times. High lands of Jaintia hills are used for betelnut or pan cultivation or as an orchard. These orchards are famous mostly for pineapples, Oranges, limes, lemons etc. Most of the farm work in slopeland orchards has been carried out manually since there is no suitable machinery. It is true that Jaintia people are generally industrious, energetic and lively. But it is now seen that most of the young Jaintias are not attracted to this kind of time consuming labourious slopeland farming. Again, there is a wide market for oranges, lemons, pineapples etc. in the entire North East. So, commercially these upland orchards are not unviable. In this paper, an attempt is made to describe how the Japanese mechanised farming system for slopeland orchard will be applicable and beneficial to highlands of Jaintia Hills.

The mechanisation of slopeland orchards with steep gradients, depends on the construction of paths for agricultural machineries. The construction of wide farm roads or paths to allow the passage of large machines is not desirable on steep slopeland. The construction cost is high and there is danger of landslides. But a new farm path system can be developed for small machines. It includes to kinds of paths, a work path which is one metre wide and a connection road with a width of more than 1.3 metre. The connection road acts as a backbone, while work paths are attached laterally to the backbone to make sure that machines can travel safely along the paths. The gradients of connection road should be less than 27%. The farm should have a turning circle where the machine can turn around. In order to prevent erosion a low cost cement aggregate pavement is developed. Such a pavement is easy to construct and the total cost is comparatively low. Construction and surfacing of a farm path is carried out as follows.

1. The path is dug out using a small back hole.
2. The cement is mixed together with the coagulant and spread over the soil surface.
3. It is mixed together with the soil using a rotary-tiller.
4. Water is sprinkled onto the mixture, using a power sprayer.

5. A rotary tiller is used to mix all the ingredients thoroughly together and smooth down the surface.

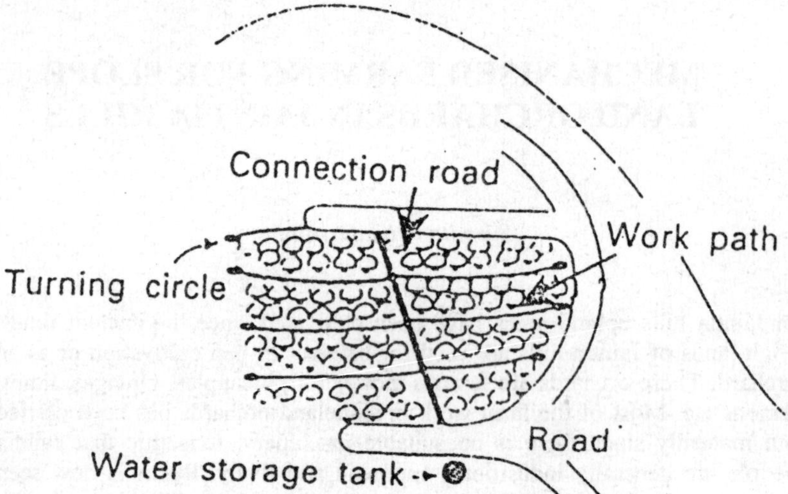

Fig. 2 : Layout of farm path system

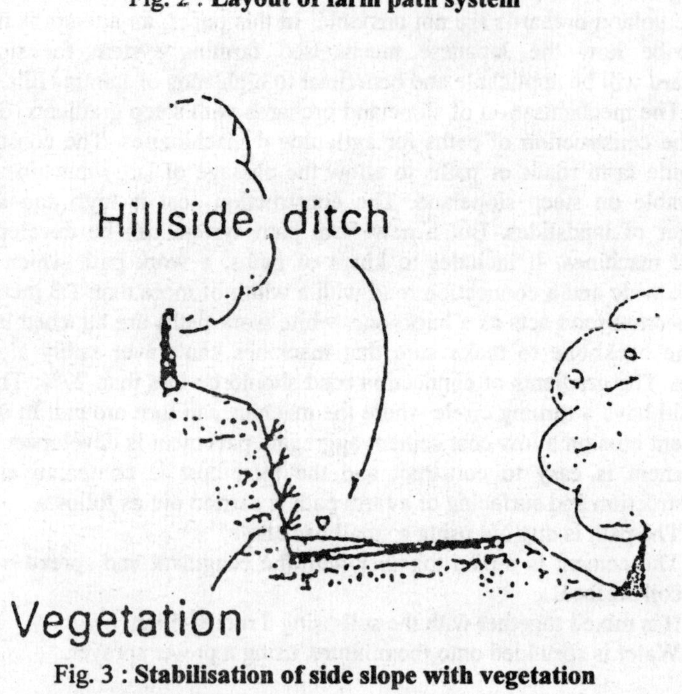

Fig. 3 : Stabilisation of side slope with vegetation

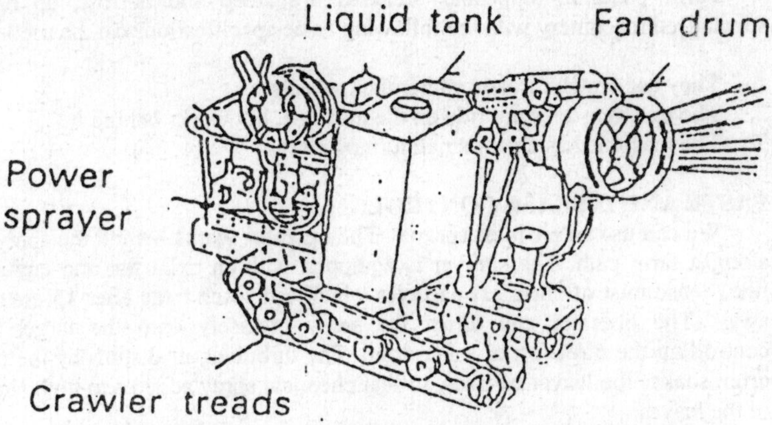

Fig. 4 : Air-blast sprayer driver by an operation on foot

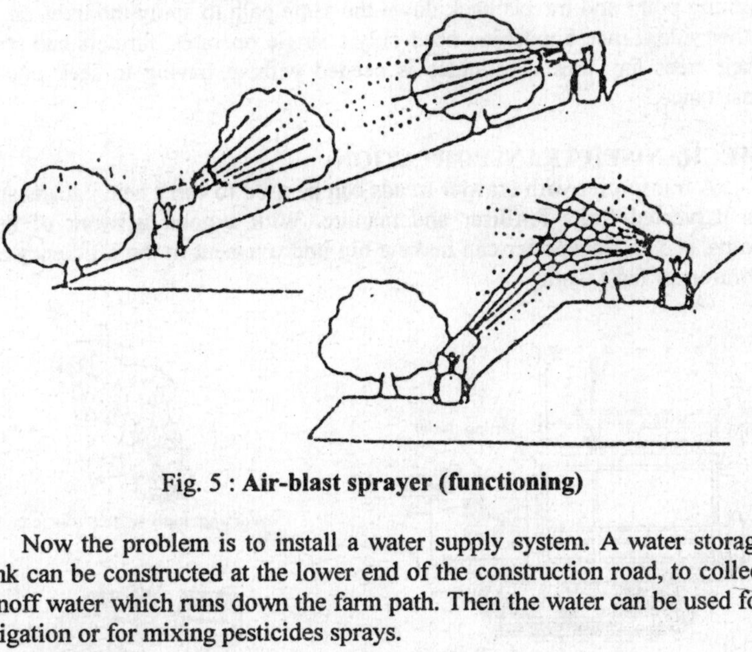

Fig. 5 : Air-blast sprayer (functioning)

Now the problem is to install a water supply system. A water storage tank can be constructed at the lower end of the construction road, to collect runoff water which runs down the farm path. Then the water can be used for irrigation or for mixing pesticides sprays.

ADVANTAGES:

1. The system not only permits the use of small machines but also improves light conditions in the lower and inner tree canopy.
2. Promotes soil conservation.

Farm paths in slopeland orchards are steep and narrow, so only specialised machinery with the following basic specifications can be used.

1. They use crawler treads, rather than wheels.
2. The operator does not ride on the machine, but works behind it.
3. The machine has a very small turning circle.

PASTE AND DISEASE CONTROL:

We can use an air-blast sprayer. The operator works behind the sprayer along a farm path. The sprayer is equipped with an axial fan and emits a fine, dense mist of chemical particles which can reach trees after 15 metres away. The operator can direct the spray precisely onto the target by controlling the direction of a fan drum. The turbulent air disturb by the fan drum shakes the leaves of trees, so that chemical spray adheres to both sides of the leaves.

One row of trees is sprayed at a time, as the machines moves along the work path. Once the row is finished, the machines turns around at the turning point and travels back down the same path to spray the trees on the other side. Since a machine need only a single operator, farmers can spray their trees any time. Pesticides is needed without having to seek outside assistance.

MECHANISED TRANSPORTATION:

A transporter with crawler treads can be used to carry heavy loads such as harvested fruits fertiliser and manure. With a good network of farm paths, such a transporter can make a big improvement in the efficiency and comfort of farm work.

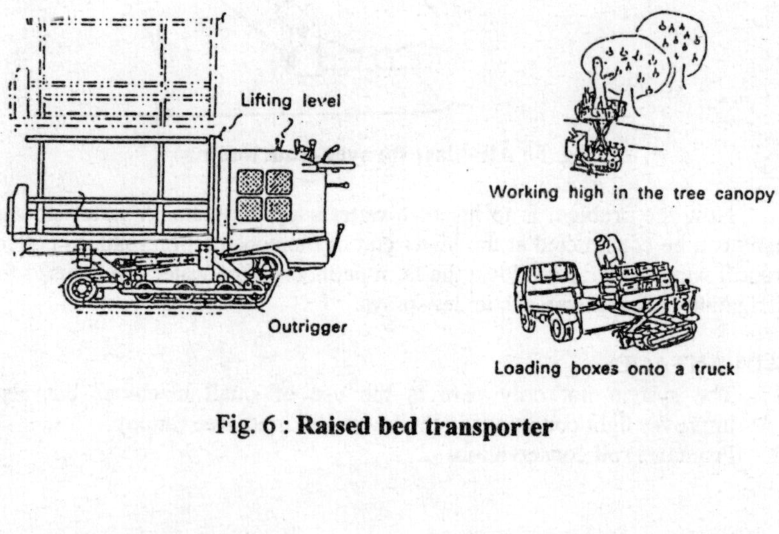

Fig. 6 : **Raised bed transporter**

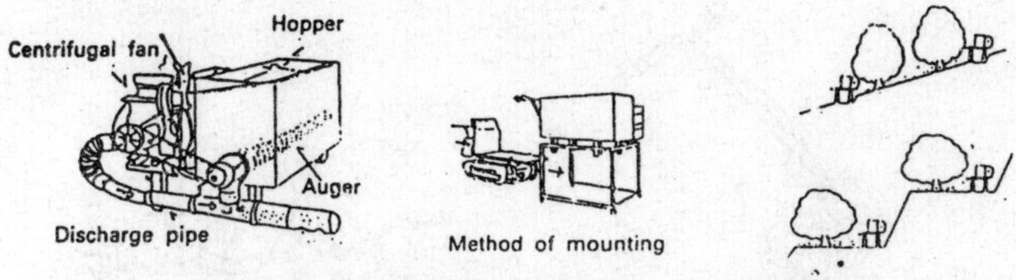

Fig. 7 : **Fertilizer unit mounted on transporter**
(Size: Length: 1.9 m, width: 0.9m, height:1.4 m,
weight: 335 kg, Discharge capacity: 14-25 kg/min)

Transporter with an adjustable elevated bed as shown in the diagram can be used. Its leading capacity is 10 container or a 200 kg. load. By raising the bed the labour of loading harvested fruit from the transporter to a truck can be reduced. In addition the raised bed can be a platform for the farmer when carrying out operation in the tree canopy, such as pruning, thinning and harvesting.

ADVANTAGE:

This transporter makes a particularly marked reduction in labour needed for transporting fruit during harvesting, so that out put of harvested fruit per worker can be increased.

MECHANISED FERTILISER APPLICATION

The worker carrying and spreading fertiliser over an orchard is not so easy. Fertiliser unit mounted on the bed of the transporter as shown in the chart can be used for this purpose. The capacity of the hopper is about 100 litres. Granular or pellet type fertiliser fed through an augar attached to the bottom of the hopper is led to discharge a pipe and blown out with air from a centrifugal fan. Mounting and unmounting unit on the bed of the transporter is easy, because of the transporter hydraulic lifting system.

Fertiliser can be applied in a bend upto 4.6 metre wide, at a rate of 14 to 25 kg/min. At this rate the operator can apply fertiliser upto 0.4 hectres per hour.

MECHANISED WEED CONTROL

For mowing weeds following three types of machines can be used:

1. Shallow cultivator: The hand-held swallow cultivator has a rotary drum fitted with a number of V-shaped claws, which can remove weeds without damaging the tree roots.

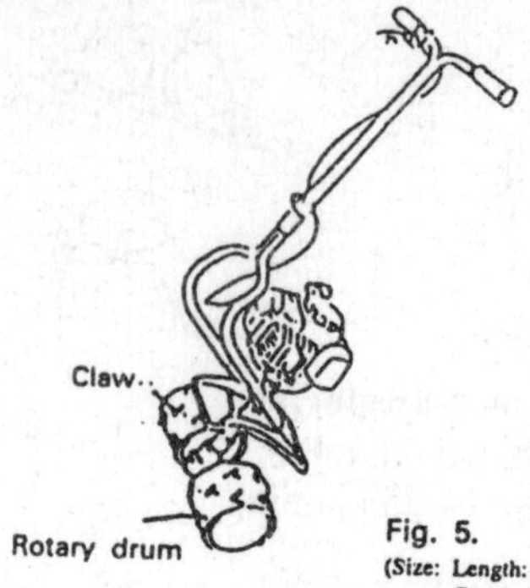

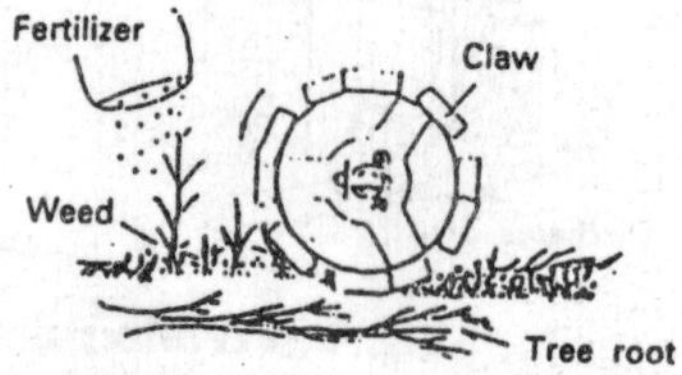

Fig. 5. Hand-held shallow cultivator
(Size: Length: 1.1 m, Width: 0.5 m, Height: 0.3 m, Weight: 12 kg. Depth of cut: 1-3 cm, width of cut: 36 cm)

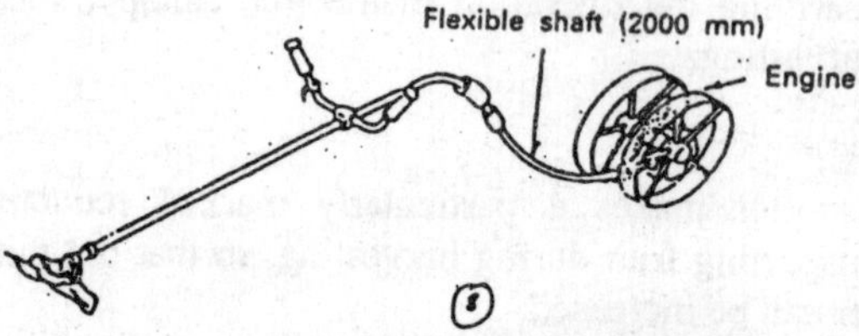

Fig. 8 : Hand-held shallow cultivator

2. Mounted cutter: The cutter has a long handle supported by a shoulder belt, with a cutting blade on the end. The handle is attached by a flexible shaft to a power unit mounted on two wheels. The power unit is pulled along the work path by the operator. Since it is mounted on two wheels, it is lighter and more comfortable than a knapsack type cutter carried on the back of the operator.
4. Rotary Mower The rotary mower have a centrifugal blade made of plastic cord. The mower is manipulated over the ground by using only one hand, in the same way as using a map to clean a floor. The operator can cut weeds under trees without bending his back.

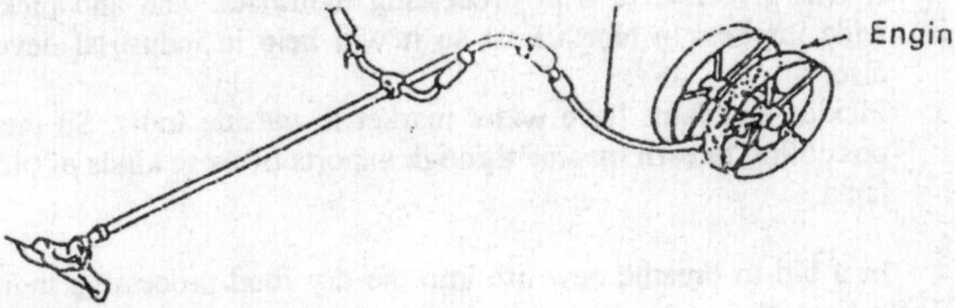

Fig. 9 : **Mounted cutter**
(Size : Length : 3.7 m. Width : 0.4 m, Height : 0.3 m, Weight : 9.9 kg)

Fig. 10 : **Rotary mower**

This mechanised farm system is practised in Japan where it has been proved to be 30% more efficient (in terms of labour hour) than the conventional method. This method has universal applicability. So I think this method can be applied in orchards of Jaintia Hills. Benefits, we can hope, from the introduction of mechanised farming in slope orchard can be summerised as follows:

1. Farmers will be able to expand the scale of their farm operations.
2. He will be able to produce high quality fruits because of the intensive care of the trees.
3. Workers will be released from much of the hard manual labour of maintaining a slopeland orchards.

4. It will give rise to fruit processing industries. Jam and pickles have wide markets in North East so it will help in industrial development also.
5. Pickles and Jams have wider market in outside India. So there is the possibility to earn income through exports of these kinds of pickles and jams.

In a bid to breathe new life into the dry food processing industries in North East, the centre has recently drawn up enhanced rates of assistance for such units. Under the provision a concessional rate of 4% soft load will be granted to all food processing units in this area, with a repayment period of 5 years after a moratorium of 1 year. Besides, the ministry also provide 75% assistance on capable cost, extending upto 100% in certain cases to such small units. So I think mechanised farming in slopeland orchard will definitely be a boon for these industries. Regarding machinery I would like to say that these machines are not costly and do not require high production cost. So mechanised farming in the slopeland orchards of Jaintias Hills will be a welcome break.

16

IMPLICATION OF COAL MINING ON ENVIRONMENT IN JAINTIA HILLS, MEGHALAYA

R K Rai

Our planet earth is perhaps a unique planet where life exists. Its physical, biological and cultural components comprise an interacting system, which is known as environment. All modern, economic, industrial and commercial activities depend mostly on the exploitation and consumption of minerals and bio resources. But the over exploitation and consumption of resources causes a wide range of environmental degradation.

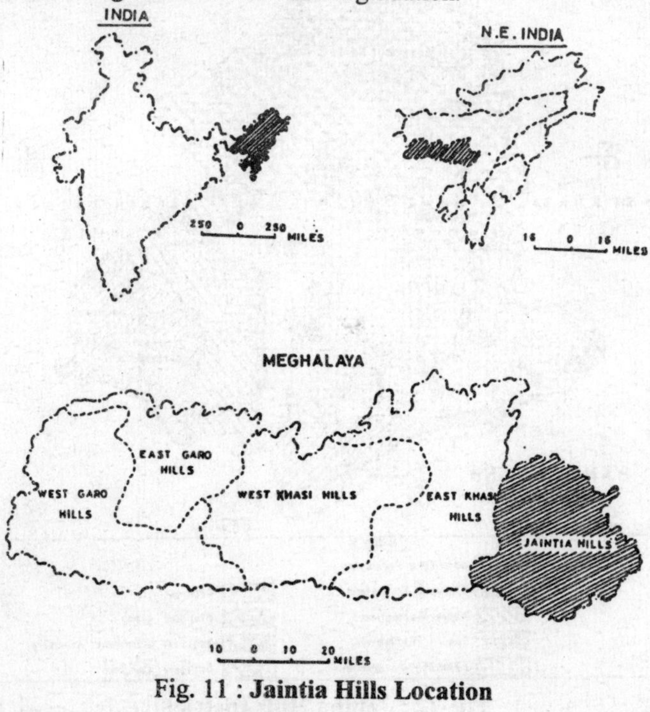

Fig. 11 : Jaintia Hills Location

The state of Meghalaya is quite rich in Tertiary coal deposits, which are confined to the upper part of the Tertiary rocks (Fig. 1). The estimated reserves of coal deposits in Meghalaya are about 600 million tones. The Jaintia Hills district is quite rich from coal deposits point of view and at present large scale extraction is going on in the district.

The coalfields of Jaintia Hills fall in the Survey of India toposheets No, 83 C/8, 83 C/7 and 83 C/11. They are small and are spread out in different patches over an area of about 75 sq. km. Tllere are nine important places of coal deposits. Out of which the Bapung and Lakadong are the important coal deposit areas. The coal deposits are found in the following places (i) Bapung (ii) Lakadong (iii) Lunshnong (iv) Malwar Musiang Lamare (v) Mutang (vi) Sutangh (vii) Jarain Tkentalang (viii) Loksi and Khaliartiat (Fig. 2).

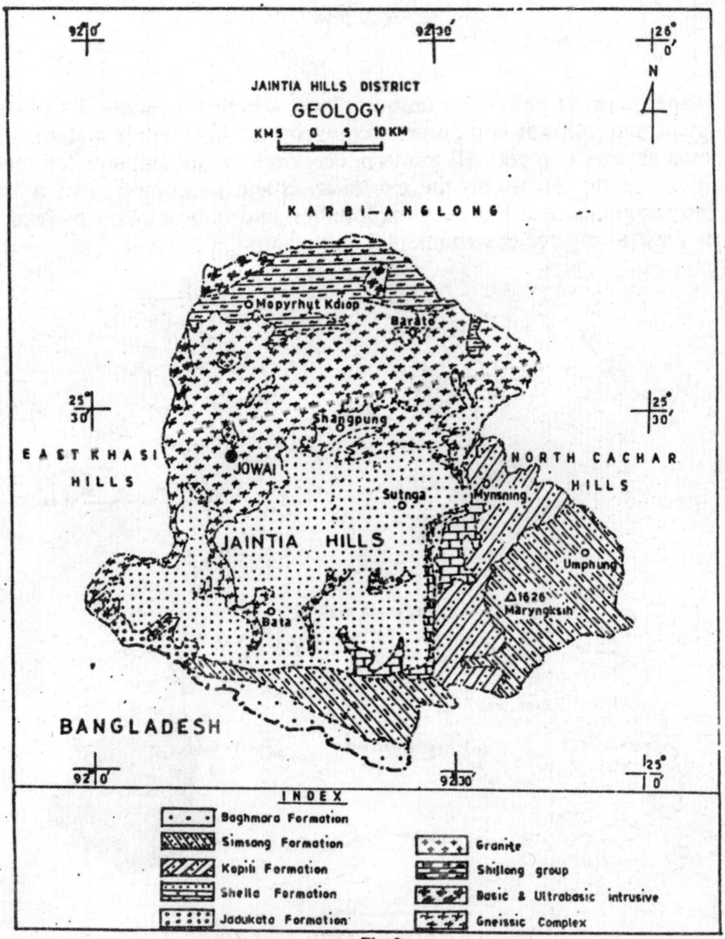

Fig. 12 : **Jaintia Hills District**

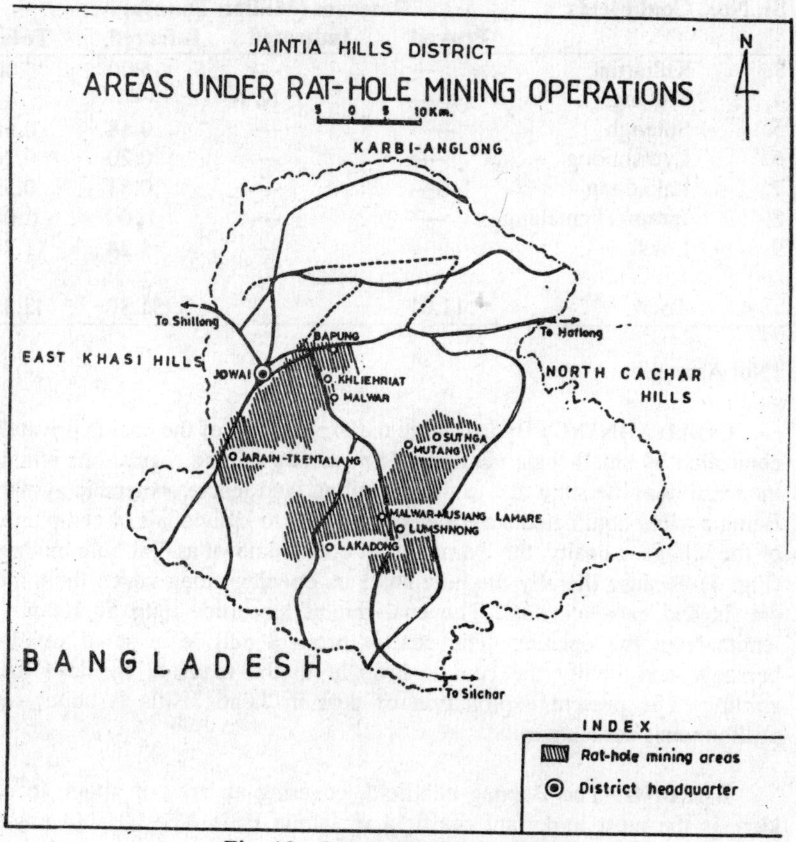

Fig. 13 : **Jaintia Hills District**

Most of the coal bearing areas can be approached by road from Jowai, the district headquarter of Jaintia Hills, located at a distance of 64 km. east of Shillong.

The NH 44 connecting Shillong, Jowai, Badarpur and Silchar leads access to Bapung, Malwar, Mutang, Lumshnong and Lakadong coalfields. The coal bearing areas of Jaintia Hills present a panorama of flat topped low hills, devoid of vegetation and a plateau of rolling grassland inter sparsed by river valleys.

Table I : Estimated coal reserves in different coalfields of Jaintia Hills

Sl. No.	**Coal Fields**	**Reserves (Million Tonnes)**			
		Proved	**Indicated**	**Inferred**	**Total**
1.	Bapung	11.01	----	22.65	33.66
2.	Malwar		N.A.*	----	----

SI. No.	Coal Fields	Reserves (Million Tonnes)			
		Proved	Indicated	Inferred	Total
3.	Khliartiat	----	----	5.00	5.00
4.	Mutang	----	N. A.	----	----
5.	Sutangh	-----	----	0.88	0.68
6.	Lymshnong	----	----	0.20	0.20
7.	Lakadong	----	----	0.53	0.53
8.	Jarain-Tkentalang	----	----	1 .00	1 .00
9.	Loksi	----	----	1.24	1.24
	Total	11.01		31.30	42.31

*Not Assessed

COAL MINING: By and large the exploitation of the coal is privately controlled by small-scale ventures. The existing mining regulations remain inoperative in the state due to the prevailing land tenure/ownership system. Being a tribal dominated state the land belongs to individuals or community or the village. Locally, the extraction of coal is known as "rat hole mining" (Fig. 3) because literally the hole has I m. opening along which the miner crawls and excavate coal. The coal miners go inside upto 50-100m. in length from the opening. The coal is brought outside in small wooden barrows, and finally the coal is brought to the roadside by head load shifting. The present exploitation of coal in Jaintia Hills is about two million tones per annum.

BAPUNG: The Bapung coalfield, covering an area of about 46 sq. kms. is the most important coalfield in Jaintia Hills. The NH- 44 passes through the heart of the coalfield connecting Jowai. The area represents a vast undulating surface with gentle slopes towards south. The general elevation varies from 1073m. to 1370m. above m.s.l. The maximum height of the hillocks is around 50m. from the valleys.

The coal seams around Bapung are hard and lumpy with moisture content varying from 1 .2 - 5.2 % on air-dried basis. The ash content varies from 5% to 20 %. The coal is high in sulphur and the total sulphur content varies from 2.9 -10.8 %.

ENVIRONMENTAL DEGRADATION

Coal mining has become one of the most important economic activity in Jaintia Hills District. It is the most profitable business in the area. But various environmental problems have cropped up in the area. The most burning problems in Jaintia Hills District due to coal mining are acute scarcity of potable water, deforestation, water pollution, land subsidence, dust pollution and increase in wasteland (Fig. 4). It is mainly because of unscientific primitive techniques and small scale coal mining.

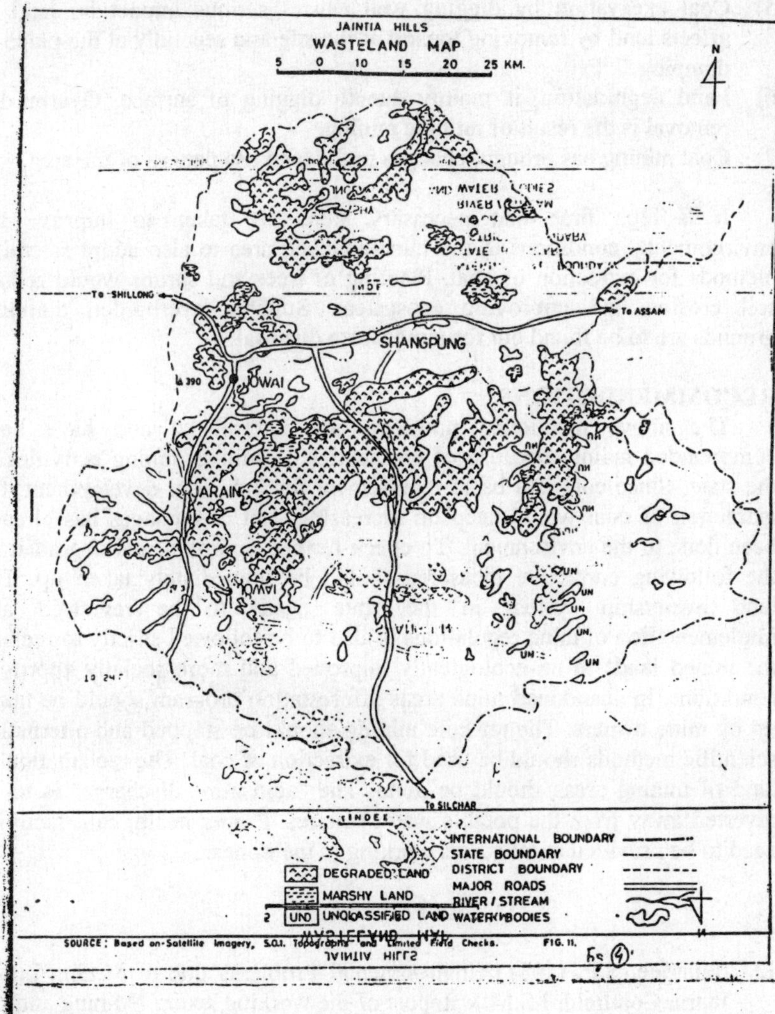

Fig. 14 : **Wasteland Map**

The main environmental problems associated with coal extraction are as follows:

1) Disturbance of land surface and underground aquifers
2) Subsidence of the land surface over underground mines.
3) Acid mine discharge.
4) Coal mining causes serious environmental problems, which has affected the vegetation, forest area and the topsoil of the area.

5) Coal excavation by digging well causes serious impact on land. It affects land by removing topsoil at the site and secondly at the place of dumping.
6) Land degradation, is mainly due to digging of surface. Overburden removal is the result of rat hole mining.
7) Coal mining has brought changes in the land use pattern of the area.

It is high time that necessary steps are taken to improve the environmental conditions in the mine-attached area to also adopt scientific methods for extraction of coal. Planting of trees and shrubs would reduce soil erosion and improving ecosystem. Suitable overburden dumping grounds are to be found out for mine waste disposal.

RECOMMENDATIONS

The above mentioned problems are interrelated and have been compounded mainly because of unscientific primitive mining activities in the state. Since coal is a basic requirement for industrial development, the extraction of coal would keep on increasing. Lot of damages has already been done to the environment. To check further environmental degradation, the following corrective measures should be immediately taken up. The land ownership system in the state needs to be reviewed and implementation of mine regulations is also to be followed strictly to reclaim the mined lands to an ecologically improved and more socially approved conditions. ln abandoned mine areas afforestation program should be taken up by mine owners. The rat hole mining should be stopped and alternative scientific methods should be used for extraction of coal. The reclamation of land of mining areas should be done. The "acid mine dlscharge" is to be diverted away from the potablc water sources. Proper health care facilities need to bc provided to labourers working in the mines.

REFERENCES

1. Banerjee, S.P. (1981) Environmental Problems due to Mining in the Jharia Coalfield, I.S.M. - Report of the working group "Mining and the Environment `` -Department af Environment, Govt. of India, New Delhi.
2. Chadwick, M.J. et al (1987) Environmental Impacts of Coal Mining; and utilisation - A complete revision of Environmental Implications of Expanded Coal Utilisation, Pergamon.press, New York, 332 p.
3. Das, A (1988) Environmental Pollution caused by Coal Minining and related industries: An Appraisal, In: (Joshi, S.C. and Bhattacharjee, G., ed.) Mining and Environment in India, H.R.G., Nainital, 108-120 p.
4. De, P. & Paul, P.K. (1989) Environmental Impact of Coal Mining on Air, Land, Water and Man - A Subjective Study, Minetech, Vol. 10, No. 5, 40-44 p.

5. Despande, A.D. & Gandhi; P.K. (1988) Coal Related activities and Environmental Pollution in India, Tr. Mine Geol. Metall. Inst. Ind., Vol. 65, No. 2, 60-70p.
6. Gogoi, K. (1975) The Geology of the Pre-Cambrian Rocks in the - Northwest part of the Khaasi and the Jaintia Hills, Meghalaya, Geol. Surv. Ind. Misc. Pub., No. 23, Pt. I, 37-48,P.
7. Ghosh, M.K. { 1989) Land Reclamation and Protection of Environment fram the effect of Coal Mining Operation, Minetech., Vol. 10; No. 5, 350-359p.

17

COAL MINING IN JAINTIA HILLS, MEGHALAYA: AN ECOLOGICAL PERSPECTIVE

S Das Gupta, B K Tiwari and R S Tripathi

ABSTRACT

The extensive unscientific mining of the coal reserves in Jaintia Hills district of Meghalaya has caused several environmental problems in the area, such as land degradation, water pollution and air pollution. The large scale dumping of consolidated and unconsolidated material overlying coal seams near the adjoining mined areas has created coal mine spoils which are generally unfavourable for growth and development of plants. Acute acidity, nutrient deficiency, sandy nature of the spoil increase in soil erosion and moisture stress characterise the mine spoil.

A study was carried out to determine the extent of damage caused to the landscape, soil, vegetation and water bodies by the mining activity in Bapung area in Jaintia Hills. The study also involved an assessment of the socio-economic status of the people directly engaged in coal mining activity as well as other residents of the area. The standard methodologies were adopted for the socio-economic survey and determination of vegetation attributes, soil characteristics and microbiological parameters. The information/ data were collected on floristic composition of the vegetation growing on degraded spoils , soil properties, nutrient concentration in soil and microbial population in soil. Based on the findings of our study,we recommend scientific management of the mines and. immediate ecorestoration of the degraded mining areas.There is a need for regular monitoring of the level of pollution in the area. It is felt that the participation of NGOs, ecologists and governmental agencies in the ecorestoration of mined areas is necessary. It is suggested that a part of the revenue earned through coal mining operations must be set aside for the rehabilitation of the coal mining affected areas. The concerted efforts of all concerned and desired level of financial input will go a long way in improving the landscape of the Bapung coal mine area in Jaintia Hills.

INTRODUCTION

Coal has been a vital energy source for mankind for centuries. It finds its use in industries, thermal power plants and as household fuel. In Jaintia Hills, coal mining is more sort of a cottage industry where coal mine owners employ manual labourers who do almost all operations using hand tools. Except a water pump used for removing water from mine wells, no other machine is used during the excavation of coal. The coal mines along with spoils are scattered all over the landscape of mining areas interspersed with agricultural fields, pine groves and human habitation. Thus all types of land use can be found in the vicinity of the coal mines. The forests, agricultural fields and grasslands dotted with coal mine spoils and coal dump are to be seen in many parts of Jaintia Hills.

Meghalaya falls under the provisions of the sixth schedule to the Indian constitution, and so, the land is solely owned by the people. The state and central governments have little control, whatsoever, on the land. The prevailing land, holding system allows the land owners to excavate coal without any restriction. Thus there are thousands of private coal mine owners who excavate coal for generating income for themselves. The excavation of coal by the private operators is done by adopting a very unscientific and obsolete method of mining known as "rat-hole" method. In this method, pits ranging from 5 to 100 m2 are dug into the soil till the coal seam is reached.The coal seam occurs at a depth ranging from 2 to 10 meters. Tunnels are made into the seam sideways and coal is brought into pits by wheel-barrows. From the pits, it is taken out in conical baskets as backloads. The columns of coal which are left during digging to serve as pillars are also cut down subsequently , as a result of which large cracks and subsidence appear on the surface of the mined land. During the digging, the pieces of rocks and soil overlying the coal seams get haphazardly mixed with small coal pieces. These waste materials are taken out and dumped near the mine sites on ground surface forming heaps or mounds of varying sizes which are referred to as coal mine spoils. These coal mine spoils represent extremely rigorous habitat for plant growth and development. Colonization, establishment and maintenance of vegetation on these spoils are extremely difficult. The present paper cavers a small part of a comprehensive investigation that was carried out to determine physico-chemical properties of coal mine spoils, to study the colonisation, establishment and growth of plants on mine spoils, and to enumerate soil microbial population and to measure the activity of soil microorganisms.

METHODS

Three coal mine spoils of varying ages, viz. 0-2 years, 6-8 years 12-14 years and an undisturbed unmined site in the vicinity were chosen in Bapung coal mine area for the study. The unmined site served as a control. Soil sayples representing O-20cm layer were collected from these sites, mixed, sieved and homogenised for determining various physico-chemical and biological characteristics of the soil.

Soil moisture was determined by drying 10 g of freshly sieved soil at 105°C for 24 hours in a hot air oven (Allen et al. 1974). Soil texture was determined by Bouyoucos hydrometer method (Allen et al. 1974) . Cation-exchange capacity (C.E.C.) was measured by the method described by Allen et al. (1974). The contents of plant nutrient elements like nitrogen (N), phosphorus (P) and potassium (K) present in the spoils were also estimated using standard methods. Microbiological analysis was done to assess the temporal variation in the population of microorganisms , viz., fungi including yeast and bacteria in the spoil and soils. The soils for microbiological examinations were collected from 0-20cm depth using sterilised spatula. The fungi were isolated by employing rose bengal agar medium (Martin, 1950) and nutrient agar medium (Johnson and Curl, 1972) was used for enumeration of bacterial colony counts.

The plant species growing on the coal mine spoils of different ages and on the unmined site were collected and identified.

The data presented in tables are means of eight determinations/ observations.

RESULTS

The analysis of soil characteristics revealed that mining has adversely affected the physico-chemical and biological characteristics of the soil, thus making it less suitable for growth and development of plants. In the newly mined spoils, soil moisture content was low because of the preponderance of gravels and rock chips which lowered the water holding capacity of the spoils. The soil moisture content showed a definite trend with the unmined control site recording the highest (52%) moisture level and the youngest mine spoil containing the least (6%) moisture. The low moisture content in coal mine spoils has been considered an important factor limiting the plant growth. The overwhelming percentage of sand was observed in the soils of all the four sites. C.E.C. showed an increasing trend with the increase in the age of the mine spoil. This could be due to a rise in clay content which provides active sites for adherence of cations. The mine spoils had inadequate nitrogen though it showed gradual increase in concentration with the increasing age of the mine spoils. The poor vegetal cover and high leaching may be responsible for low N-concentrations. Phosphorus and potassium were extremely low in all the mine spoil sites which could be ascribed to the leaching and lack of binding power in the soil. Gradual increase was observed in N, P and K concentrations with the increasing age of the mine spoil, which shows that a recovery has occurred. The organic-carbon content varied from 22mg/g in the unmined control site to 3mg/g in the youngest mine spoil (Table 1).

The bacterial and fungal populations were maximum in the soils of the unmined control site whereas the mine spoils, in general, had a very low microbial population. This could be attributed to the significantly low organic-C content of the mine spoils, which however, builds up with the increasing age of the spoil. The youngest mine spoil showed a very low microbial population which might have been caused due to harsh microenvironmental conditions lilce direct sunlight and low relative humidity (Table 2).

Table-31 : Physico-chemical properties of soils from the coal mine spoils of different ages and the unmined control site.

Parameters	Control	12-14 year old spoil	6-8 year old0-2 spoil	year old spoil
Soil Moisture (%)	52	22	10	6
Sand(%)	97	84	82	93
CEC ml/100g	9.0	2.0	1.0	0.8
N (mg/g)	2.0	1 .0	0.5	0.2
P(mg/g)	0.30	0.02	0.02	0.01
K(mg/g) x 10^{-3}	0.24	0.17	0.10	0.0
Organic-C (mg/g)	22	15	9	3

Table-32 : Bacterial and fungal populations (numbers per g dry wt. of soil) in the coal mine spoils of different ages and the unmined control site.

Parameters	Control	12-14 year ohd spoil	6-8 year old spoil	0-2 year old spoil
Bacterial population(x 10^4)	15	10	7	4
Fungal population	2751	1788	1038	262

The vegetation development on the mine spoils was very much related to their age. The maximum number (39) of plant species was recorded from the unmined control site, whereas on the 0-2 year old spoil, only 2 plant species were observed to grow. With the increase in the age of the mine spoils the number of plant species growing on them increased. For example, in the 6-8 year old spoil, the number was 13 and on the 12-14 year old spoil, it was 28 (Table 3). The number of herbs was more than the shrubs in all the sites studied (Table 3). The plant species that were found growing on the mine spoils are listed in Table 4 . Certain plant species such as Gnaphalium luteo-album, Oxalis corniculata, Polygonum capitatum and Pteris seem to have preference for the mine spoils. Some of the plant species which are well adapted to grow on these mine spoils are Borreria hispida, Arundinella khasiana and Dicranopteris linearis.

Table-33 : Number of species of herbs and shrubs growing on the coal mine spoils of different ages and the control site.

Species Groups	Control	12-14 years old spoil	6-8 years old spoil	0-2 years old spoil
Herbs	30	24	11	2
Shrubs	9	4	2	-
Total	39	28	13	2

Table-34 : Important plant species found growing on the mine spoils of different ages and the control site.

Sl. No.	Name of the species	Control	12-14 year old spoil	6-8 year old spoil	0-2 year old spoil
1.	Arundinella khasiana	+	+	+	-
2.	Arisaema tortuosum	+	-	-	-
3.	Ageratum conyzoides	+	-	-	-
4.	Anaphalis linearis	+	-	-	-
5.	Ainsliaea latifolia	+	-	-	-
6.	Axonopus compressus	+	+	+	-
7.	Borreria hispida	+	+	-	-
8.	Centella asiatica	+	-	+	-
9.	Commelina bengalensis	+	+	-	-
10.	Crossocephalum Crepidioides	+	+	-	-
11.	Crotolaria sp.	+	-	-	-
12.	Cyanotis vaga	+	+	+	-
13.	Dicranopteris linearis	+	+	+	+
14.	Drymeria cordata	+	+	-	-
15.	Eleusine nigra	+	+	-	-
16.	Eupatorium adenophorum	+	+	-	-

Sl. No.	Name of the species	Control	12-14 year old spoil	6-8 year old spoil	0-2 year old spoil
17.	Gnaphalium luteo-album	-	+	+	-
18	Hedyotis macrophylla	+	+	-	-
19.	Houttuynia cordata	+	+	-	-
20.	Hydrocotyle javanica	+	-	-	-
21.	Hypochaeris radicata	+	+	+	-
22.	Impatiens khasiana	+	-	-	-
23.	Imperata cylindrica	+	+	+	-
24.	Lantana camara	+	-	-	-
25.	Lindernia Sp.	+	-	-	-
26.	Lycopodium clavatum	+	+	+	-
27.	Melastoma sp.	+	+	-	-
28.	Mosses and other bryophytes	+	+	+	+
29.	Oxalis corniculata	-	+	-	-
30.	Osbeckia stellata	+	+	+	-
31.	Paederia foetida	+	+	+	-
32.	Pratia begonifolia	+	+	-	-
33.	Paspalum orbiculare	+	+	-	-
34.	Phyllanthus urinaria	+	+	-	-
35.	Plantago major	+	-	+	-
36.	Plectranthus striatus	+	+	-	-
37.	Polygonum capitatum	-	+	-	-
38.	Pteris Sp.	+	+	+	+
39.	Rubus alceifolious	+	-	-	-
40.	Senecio densiflorus	+	-	-	-

+ present; - absent.

The study suggests that subsequent to coal mining, the physico-chemical and biological characteristics of soils become unfavourable for plant growth and development. However, the mine spoils gradually and steadily recovered and in about fourteen years time , the soils regained most of their vital attributes. The process of ecorestoration however, can be hastened by suitable intervention by way of planting leguminous species on the spoils. As reported by Lyngdoh (1995), a leguminous plant viz., Eriosaema chinense is found to grow frequently in the coal mine area of Jarain in the Jaintia Hills district and according to her, this plant by virtue of nodulating profusely and by showing its ability to grow on the soils collected from the mine spoils, is likely to play a significant role in nitrogen economy of the soil. Similarly, other suitable leguminous plants could also be identified for ecorestoration of the mine spoils.

The colonisation of coal mine spoils by plant species has been considered to be one of the important ways of their rehabilitation. The rhizomatous and stoloniferous grass species such as Axonopus compressuss, Chrysopogon gryllus and Arundinella nepalensis which have been observed to grow successfully on the spoils by Lyngdoh et al. (1992) can be useful. Of these three grasses, Axonopus compressus has a perennial stolon in which rooting takes place at the nodes. This growth characteristic, as observed by Lyngdoh et al.(1992), helps bind the soil particles thus making the loose mine spoils more stable and less prone to soil erosion.

Based on the above research findings, we suggest the introduction of scientific method of coal mining in the area and scientific disposal of mine water as well as spoils. Adequate care needs to be taken to prevent and minimise land subsidence after mining. This could be done by refilling of the excavated mines with mine spoils or top soils. This can be followed up with a scheme to revegetate the mine spoils with acid-tolerant species including leguminous plants. Dust reduction technique can be effectively utilised during coal loading and transportation to bring down the level of air pollution .The quality of land and water, flora and fauna (including stream fishes) of the mine affected area needs to be improved subsequent to the initial ecorestoration works.This can be achieved by entrusting the Meghalaya State Pollution Control Board with the task of conducting periodic analysis of water, soil and air samples from the coal mining areas. The local village leaders need to be educated about the damage that coal mining activity causes to the adjoining areas. A village level committee may be constituted for monitoring the coal mining activity with a view to protecting water sources and paddy tields. As suggested by Uma Shankar et al. (1993), the seepage water from the mined areas should be properly channelised to stop deterioration of soil quality in agricultural fields and low lying marginal lands. The mine owners should set aside a part of their income for the restoration of the degraded mined lands. The state government and district councils also earn revenue from the coal mining, and as such they have a moral responsibility to plough-back a part of this revenue towards the management of coal mining and ecorestoration of mining affected areas as well as for the welfare of mine labourers. The state department of Mining and Geology should expose the mine owners with latest mining technologies and pursuade them to adopt the appropriate ones. This will be a useful step towards introducing scientific mining and preventing pollution. Suitable health schemes should be launched to prevent the spread of skin diseases, heart and lung problems, whooping cough etc. among the mine labourers. Insurance cover for mine workers should also be provided. An attempt should be made to bring scientific information and technology to the doorstep of the residents of coal mining areas particularly those who are engaged in mining activity to enable them to use the appropriate technologies for preventing environmental degradation and health hazards. The present study reinforces that the ecorestoration through natural reclamation as advocated by Tiwari (1996), may be successful under the conditions obtaining in Jaintia Hills. A field trial for the ecorestoration of these degraded areas needs to be conducted and a suitable demonstration model should be developed for its adoption by the coal miners of this area.

ACKNOWLEGEMENT

The authors are thankful to the Head, Department of Botany, NEHU, for providing laboratory facilities for conductance of this study.

REFERENCES

1. Allen, S.K.; Grimshaw, H.M.; Parkinson, J. A. and Quarmby, C. 1974. Chemical Analysis of Ecological Materials. Blackwell Scientific Publications . Oxford, England
2. Johnson, L.F. and Curl, E.A. 1972. Methods for the Research On Ecology Of Soil-borne Plant Pathogens. Burgess Publishing Co., Minneapolis. pp. 247.
3. Lyngdoh T. (1995). Community Dynamics and Edaphic Changes in Relation to Coal Mining In Jaintia Hills, Meghalaya. Ph.D. thesis, North-Eastern Hill University. Shillong.
4. Lyngdoh, T., Tripathi, R.S. and Das, A.K. (1992). Vegetation dynamics on coal mine spoils of Jaintia Hills in Meghalaya (North-east India) undergoing natural recovery. Acta Oecologica, 13 (6): 767-775.
5. Martin, J.P. 1950. Use of Acid, Rose Bengal and Streptomycin In Plate Method for Estimating Soil Fungi, Soil Science, 69 : 215-232 .
6. Shankar. U. Boral, L., Pandey, H.N. and Tripathi, R.S. (1993). Degradation of Land Due to Coal Minining and Its Natural Recovery Pattern. Current Science, 65(9): 680-687.
7. Tiwari, B.K. (1996). Impact of coal mining on ecosystem health in Jaintia Hills, Meghalaya. In Conservation and Management of Biological Resources in Himalaya. (eds.)
9. P.S.Rama Krishnan et al. pp. 465-475. G.B.Pant Institute, Almora and Oxford IBH Co., New Delhi.

18

Contribution of the Missionaries Towards Development of Education In Jaintia Hill Areas of Meghalaya

K. S. Lyngdoh
A. Henia

INTRODUCTION

Education has continued to evolve, diversify and extend its reach and coverage since the dawn of human history. Every country develops its system of education to express and promote its unique socio-cultural identity and also to meet the challenges of the times. It is a fact that education is one of the most powerful medium that can change and transform a society to greater heights and development. Education is needed for all and must be extended to even the remotest corner of the country. This brings the justification of a person fundamental rigid to education and equality of educational opportunity.

JAINTIA HILLS MEGHALAYA

Jaintia Hills constitute one of the current Districts of Meghalaya and is predominantly inhabited bg the Jaintia people. During the British colonial period in India, the district used to be callad jointly as the Khasi and Jaintia Hill Area under Assam Province Administration. This system contained till statehood formation in 1972. With the emergence of Meghalaya as a separate state under the North East Reorganisation act of 1971-72, Govt. of India, `Jaintia Hills' has been created as a separate district and continued till date.

POLITICAL DEVELOPMENT OF THE JAINTIAS

The British contact with the Khasi & Jaintia Hills started around 1820 through David Scott (British Official). The tribes were subjugated and compelled to accept the supremacy of the British and a series of agreement were concluded. The subjugation of the Khasi Hills was due to the fact that there was disunity among the rulers-village chiefs. But the most important factor was British superior organization and arms. Thus, the entire Khasi and Jaintia Hills came under the control of the British.

The Jaintias were ruled by their own 'Syiems' or Raas. The office of the Jaintia System existed till 1835 where Jaintia Hills was occupied by the British. Then it was placed under the political officer of the Khasi Hills and the direct management was vested in an Assistant who was stationed at Jowai. Jowai developed as the administrative headquarters and in course of time it became the cultural headquarters of Jaintia Hills. It is viewed that political, social, cultural and economic modernization of the Jaintias began in Jowai which started to develop as the first urban centre in the District and the process of change gradually infiltrated into the rural areas. In the beginning the British followed the policy of 'non-interference in the 'Jaintia Hills' but later on adopted changes in their policy. Chiefly due to Jaintias revolt against the British Authority in the 1860. The uprising was alleged to have been the result of interference with the indigenous tribes' socio-religious practices and others, which according to the British officials was inhuman and severe. Finally Cecil Beaton, Lieutenant Governor of Bengal presidency at the time conducted to lay down the plan for reconstruction of the administration system of the Jaintia Hills in 1863. Simultaneously the British Govt. adopted firm measures for suppression of this cruel socio-religions practices of the Jaintias. A change in political and administrative system occurred in Khasi and Jaintia Hills durin 1874 where Assam was separtaed from that of Bengal Presidency and constituted into a separate province under a chief commissioner. With this the Khasi and Jaintia Hill areas were put under Assam province administration system and immediately made the headquarters of the province. In this way the hills were integrated with the plains districts of Assam and Surma Valley. It had broaden the outlook of the tribe and isolation of the Jaintias was observed less, active business transaction carried out between the hill tribes and the plain areas.

The Advent of Christian Missions in the North East and Khasi-Jaintia Hill areas :

In the 19th Century Christian Missions attd Colonialism seemed to follow upon each other in Africa and Asia. In the beginning entry of the various Christian missions into the North East Region was not under the dictate of the Imperial direction. It was purely the outcome of the individual enterprise and effort in association with Wastern Christian Missions to bring the light of the Gospel to the tribes. Thus Evangelization and preaching was their main focus, soon they realised that such activities could not be fulfilled nor the target could be reached without basic litracy ability on the part of the people. Because they must know how to read and understand the words of the Gospel (The Bible) and confirm their faith.

On the other hand the British Officials were finding difficult to control over their subjects due to poor, uncivilzed and illiterate conditions of the people, Curiously enough, the initiative for starting missionary enterprise also came from the Govt. officials in all the North East Region. This was so, because of the realisation of the futility of the policy of Military Expedition in the hill areas. Obviously they found the opportunity in the missionaries whose main activity was evangelisation/preaching, education and welfare. In the meantime colonial power was benefited as they could launched their expansionist policy in the North East Frontier with the help of educated natives.

The various missions along with their missionaries that came to the hills of Khasi and Jaintia were the following :

(A) THE SERAMPARE BAPTIST MISSION

The missionaries who associated this Mission was William Cary and Krishna Chandra Pal, who was also one of the pioneer. By 1838 the British Missionary society decided to hand over its two regions Assam and Arakan to the American Baptish Mission. Thus Serampare Mission was amalgamated with the Baptist Missionary society.

(B) WELSH CALVINISTIC METHODISTS FOREIGN MISSION NOW (WELSH PRESBYTERIAN CHURCH)

In 1795, the London Missionary society was established. The Calvinistic Methodist continued their connection with the London Missionary society until 1840. The Presbyterian Church in North East India had its beginning in 1841, when Thomas Jones the first Missionary of the Welsh Calvinistic Methodist Foreign Mission arrived at Cherrapunjee. Other missionaries who came and worked in the Khasi and Jaintia Hills were such as :

Alexander Lish of Cary's London missionary society, 1832, Thomas Jons-I – 1841. Thomas Jones - II, Hugh Robert Rev. Robert, John Robert, E.H. William, Rev. J.C. Evans, Dr. Griffith Hughes, Rev (Dr) Edward William and Mrs. William Rev. & Mrs. R. David Jones, Rev, John Jones and Mrs. John, Dr. & Mrs. D. Arthur Huges. This Mission contributed a lot to promotion of literacy ability and medical welfare as well as educational growth in the area.

(C) ROMAN CATHOLIC CHURCH MISSION :

Catholic Missionaries came much later in the North East. Its world Organization Headquarters is located in Rome, Italy. This mission entered into the hills of Khasi & Jaintia Hill in 1890. The German Salvadorian Missionaries (1890-1915) were the first Catholic Missionaries to venture into the land Fr. C. Becker (1906) was a prominent missionary in this mission. The Catholic Church mission educational enterprise is incomparable. Today their educational institution contributions are excellent and outstanding. They are even maintaining hospitals.

(D) THE SEVENTH DAY ADVENTIST CHURCH MISSION

This mission entered into the hill areas of Khasi & Jaintia. This church too establishes Schools. It also runs a training institute at Jowai.

MISSIONARY EFFORTS TOWARDS EDUCATIONAL DEVELOPMENT IN JAINTIA HILL AREAS.

The establishment of Imperial expansion was invariably followed by the advent of Western Christian Missionaries who took upon themselves the task of educating the people, and preaching the Gospel. Education and Evangelization of the tribe went hand-in-hand. One of the first thing they started was to learn the local dialects, put them into writing in Roman script. Produced Primers for the schools which they started at their own initiative translated the Bible into vernacular dialect alongside other primary works ultimately resorted to creative literary writings. Thus the Cherra dialect became the standard Khasi for literature nad was applied all over Khasi and Jaintia hills.

Development of education in Jaintia hills was at a slow pace, the Welsh Presbyterian Mission established the first primary school in 1854 at Jowai. This marked the beginning of educational development in Jaintia Hills. Notable native teachers was U Luh in the area apart from the other missionaries. Next another school was opened at Lamin in 1859 later at Shangpung, Nongbah and Nongtaland in 1864. Further progress was halted due to mass revolt in Jaintia Hills (1862-64) or Anglo-Jaintia war against the British Government. At that time strong superstitious attitude coming out of their socio cum religious practices and misgivings prevailed about the schools that were set up by the foreign missionaries. Parents were against sending their children to such institution due to ignorance and illiteracy on their part. The worse was that girls education was considered a taboo later this inhibition was removed by the missionary's wives effort and encouragement, children attendance was irregular, unruly and they use to run away from the classroom when corrections were made. Their behaviour was wild, in course of timethings became better. In order to encourage education, teachers adopted various other measures and techniques such as giving incentives in the form of money or garment to the students.

For a time the missionaries were seriously handicapped by such opposition of the people, coupled by their own problems of non-availability of fund created a blow to their effort. Consequently severe presecution in various forms on the missionaries and native converts were carried out by the indigenous native people. It was not a bed of roses for the missionaires to work among the hostile, unruly and uncivilized society (at the time), steeped with heathen worship. It was a life of physical hardships and mental and psychological tensions for them, the Missionaries and their native convert friends were severaly presecuted by compelling them to leave the village, denied of food supply for their need, their small hut and houses including mission offices were frequently attacked and burnt down. They lived under constant threat of being killed, social alleniation on the native converts by their own people exists just because they adopted Christianity as their religion. In this way Missionaries endured all kinds of hardships and personal sacrifices for the cause of bringing the Gospel light and upliftment of the tribesmen.

On the whole outbreak of Jaintia Rebellion was indeed a direct challenge to the imperial authority in the hills. But to the missionaries under such circumstances it was a time of trial and test to pursue their objective i.e. to Preach the Gospel to all Nations and Tribesmen, to Educate and develop the tribes urging them to shun from any unhealthy, prejudiced social and religions practices of the area.

When such turbulent period subsided, then only the Jaintia people realised and appreciated the benefits of the school. The British Govt. too appreciated the efforts of the missionaries by giving financial grant to the mission school. Such support and help enabled the Welsh Presbyterian Mission to gradually establish a school each, at least in all the important villages of Jaintia Hills.

The schools were all primary type, later Middle Schools were set up at Jowai and Shangpung. The Presbyterian Middle English School was upgraded in to a High School in 1941. In the very first year of its upgradation, the school had only 6 classes that is, from Class III to Class VIII with 167 pupils. Gradually students enrollment increased and by 1947 there were about 240 studnets in the school each year class upgradation system upto Matric Standard followed leading towards building up of colleges in the area. The first batch of the school appeared the Matriculation examination under the Gauhati University in 1944 since then they continued to appear the Matriculation examination till 1962 when it was repalced by the Higher Secondary Board of Examination – Assam.

Subjects taught in the school were the following :

Classes

III – VI : English, Vernacular dialect, Arithmetic, Geometry, History, Geography, Hygiene, Drawing, Handwriting, Hand work and sewing.

VI – X : English, Vernacular dialect, Mathematics, History, Geography, Commercial Geography, Hygiene, Science and Additional Mathematics.

The Catholic Mission established the St. Mary Mazzarello School at Jowai in 1926. By 1931 there were about 87 schools managed by different organisation in the Jaintia Hill area. The adventist Mission established the Adventist Training School at Jowai, this was known in the initial stage as Assam Training School – was a purely private school managed by its own mission. This was started by Pastor O.W. Lange. It imparted academic knowledge as well as vocational training too. The curriculum were of the following : Cultivation & farming system, Training in dairying and Pasteurization, driving lesson and Mechanical repair besides other mechanical courses and for girls sewing, needle work &other etc.

MEDIUM OF INSTRUCTION

English was used as the only medium of instruction in some schools e.g. (Adventist Training School). Other schools in the distirct used vernacular dialect in Roman letter (Khasi dialect Cherra) and English as the medium of instruction. However for the high school section, English was adopted as the medium of instruction and Khasi dialect was studied as a vernacular subject.

The literacy percentage in 1901 was 5.67% whichincreased to 9.24% in 1931.

The Catholic missionaries started their pioneering work in the region by 1910. But they came out as a major force of bringing good educational standard in the area. Prominent missionary like Rev. D.E. Becker is worth to be acknowledged and metioned in this context.

CONCLUSIONS

Development of Education in the Jaintia Hill areas was chiefly contributed by the Christian missions such as the Welsh Presbyterian, Roman Catholic, Seventh Day Adventist. The Missionaries effort and sacrifices led to the growth of education and modernisation in the area. Had it not been their contribution perhaps today the scenario of the Jaintia may be different and undeveloped.

REFERENCES

1. S. R. Vashisht & Rani P. Sharma, *Education in India,* Delhi, 1997.
2. Becker, C., *History of the Catholic Mission in North-East India,* Shillong, 1980.
3. Mackengie, Alexander, *History of the relations of Government with the Hill tribes of the North-East Frontier of Bengal,* Calcutta, 1884.
4. Morris, J. H., *The History of the Welsh Calvinistic Methodists Foreign Mission,* Liverpool, 1910.
5. Allen, B. C., *Assam District Gazetteer,* Vol. X (Gazetteer of the Khasi & Jaintia Hills), Delhi, 1905.
6. Sen, S. P. (ed.), *Social and Religions Reform Movement in the 19th and 20th Centuries,* Calcutta, 1979.
7. Barpujari, H. K., *Problems of the Hill Tribe, North East Frontier (1843-1872),* Vol. II, Gauhati, 1976.

19

LITERACY SCENARIO IN JAINTIA HILLS DISTRICT, MEGHALAYA

P. Devi

INTRODUCTION

Jaintia Hills district is one of the seven districts of Meghalaya lying between 25° 05' N to 25° 45' N latitudes and 91° 58' E to 92° 47' E longitudes. It covers an area of about 3819 sq. km. Which is bounded by the International boundary with Bangladesh in its south, while it is bounded by the state boundary with Assam in its northern and eastern side. The western side of Jaintia Hills district is bounded by the district boundary of the East Khasi Hills district. The district consists of four community Development blocks viz. Thadlaskein, Laskein, Amlaren and Khliehriat

ORIGIN OF THE JAINTIAS

According to historian, the Jaintias are the stock of Mon-Khamer people of Mongoloid race and are Austric by their linguistic affiliation. They resemble with the Mon-Khamer people in some basic characteristics of language, festivals and in erecting stone monoliths etc. Therefore, it could be said that the Jaintias may have come from the South East first to the splendid valley of Assam and then the Meghalaya.[1] The people who inhabit the Jaintia Hills district are known as *'Syntengs'*. According to Dr. Suniti Kumar Chatterjee, the renouned historian, the word 'Jaintia' *(Zantain or Zonten)* was derived from the word *'Synteng' B Pakem*[2] being a Jaintia himself said that the word 'Synteng' is derived from *'Sutnga' (Suteng),* the ruling dynasty of the Jaintias or from the word *'Sohkynting' (Smynting or Synting)* a village through which the Khasis came to the Jaintia Hills. The term *'Teng'* means the ancient mother and therefore *'Syntengs'* means the children of the ancestral mother. Jaintias seem to have an organisation and the original Khasi word *'Synteng' (Zeinten)* developed into Jaintia[3]. G. Paul[4] wrote in his book that the Jaintias were the original inhabitants of a State in the Chinese region called *'T' sin-tiang.* This is an Austric word and the people of this state were called *'T' sin'tiang* or *'T' sin-tien.* In course of time they came to be known as *'Synteng'* or *'Syntein'.*

LITERACY SCENARIO

The educational institutions which are primarily responsible for liteacy rate are not adquate to achieve satisfactory level. The first educational institution was opened in 1854 by the Welsh Mision with Government aid at Jaintia Hills district.[5] The primary education has been transferred from the Government of Assam to the United Khasi and Jaintia Hills Autonomous District Council on the 1st April, of 1962. It has been handed over to the Jaintia Hills District Council on the April 1967.[6] At present there are 466 primary and 82 middle basic schools in the rural areas of inhabited villaes in Jaintia Hills district. Jowai, the district head quarter along has 17 primary and 6 middle schools. On the other hand there are 27 High Schools and 3 Higher Secondary Schools in the district. In addition, there are 170 Adult Literacy Centres, 32 Rural Functional Literacy Project (RFLP), 70 State Adult Education Project (SAEP, Anganwadi centres, 274 and Voluntary organisations/Mahila Samities 116 also rendered services to the rural illiterates of the district (Table :1)

Table 35 : Formal and Non-formal Educational Organisations in Jaintia Hills District of Meghalaya

Sl. No.	Types of Institutions	No. of Institutions Rural	Urban	Total
A.	**Formal Educational Institutions**			
	1. Primary School	466	17	483
	2. Middle Basic School	82	6	88
	3. High School	24	3	27
	4. Higher Secondary School	2	1	3
B.	**Non-Formal Educational Institutions**			
	1. Primary Non-formal Educational Centre	-	-	135
	2. Adult Educational Centre	-	-	170
	3. Janashiksha Nilayam Centre	-	-	NA
	4. Rural Functional Literacy Project (RFLP) Centre	-	-	32
	5. State Adult Education Project (SAEP) Centre	-	-	70
	6. Anganwadi Centre	-	-	274
	7. Voluntary Organisation/Mahila Samityies	-	-	116

Source : Project Fromulation for the TLC in Jaintia Hills Disrict, Meghalaya

The data available from the District census Handbook, Jaintia Hills, reveals that there are as many as 95 villages which do not have any school facilities. The block wise break up of different blocks shows that in

Thadlaskein C.D. Blocks, 26 villages donot have school facilities. Likewise Lakein too has 18 villages, Khliehriat, 35 villages and Amlarem block 16 villages, which are not served by any school. The total illiterates accounts 1,99,872 in five C.D. blocks of Jaintia Hill district of Meghalaya. As per 1991 census the literacy rates of the district is far below (35.32%) than the state average (49.10%) and national average (52.21%0, Table : II.

Table 36 : Literacy Rates and Sex Difference in Jaintia Hills District of Meghalaya

Sl. No.	Country/State/ District/Block	Literacy Rates			Sex Difference	
		Total	Male	Female	Male	Female
	India	52.21	64.13	39.29	24.84	
	Meghalaya	49.10	52.12	44.85	7.27	
	Jaintia Hills	35.32	34.37	36.31		1.94
1.	Thadlaskein C.D.	42.15	40.96	43.32		2.36
2.	Amlarem C.D.	40.80	41.48	40.09	1.39	
3.	Laskein C.D.	30.35	25.89	37.74		11.85
4.	Khliehriat C.D.	28.06	29.30	26.66	2.64	

The Block wise literacy rates in Jantia Hills district shows that Thadlaskein block has the highest literacy rates of 42.15 per cent, Amlarem 40.80 per cent, Lakein 30.35 per cent and Khliehriat has the lowest literacy rate of 28.06 per cent among all the four blocks (Figure 1). Significantly it is the only district in the whole India, which ha shigher female literacy rates (36.31%) than the males (34.37%). Block level data on female literacy reveals that the Laskein is the highest female literate block of Jaintia Hills district of Meghalaya where sex difference is 11.85 per cent. On the other hand Thadlaskein block shows 2.36 per cent more female literates than males (Figure 2).

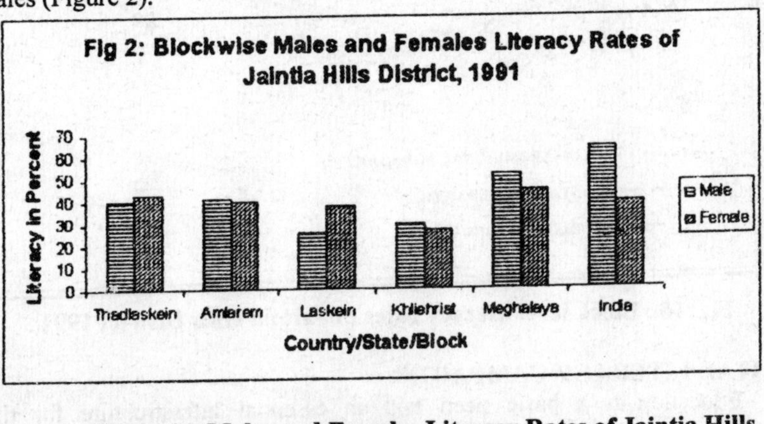

Fig. 15 : **Blockwise Males and Females Literacy Rates of Jaintia Hills District, 1991**

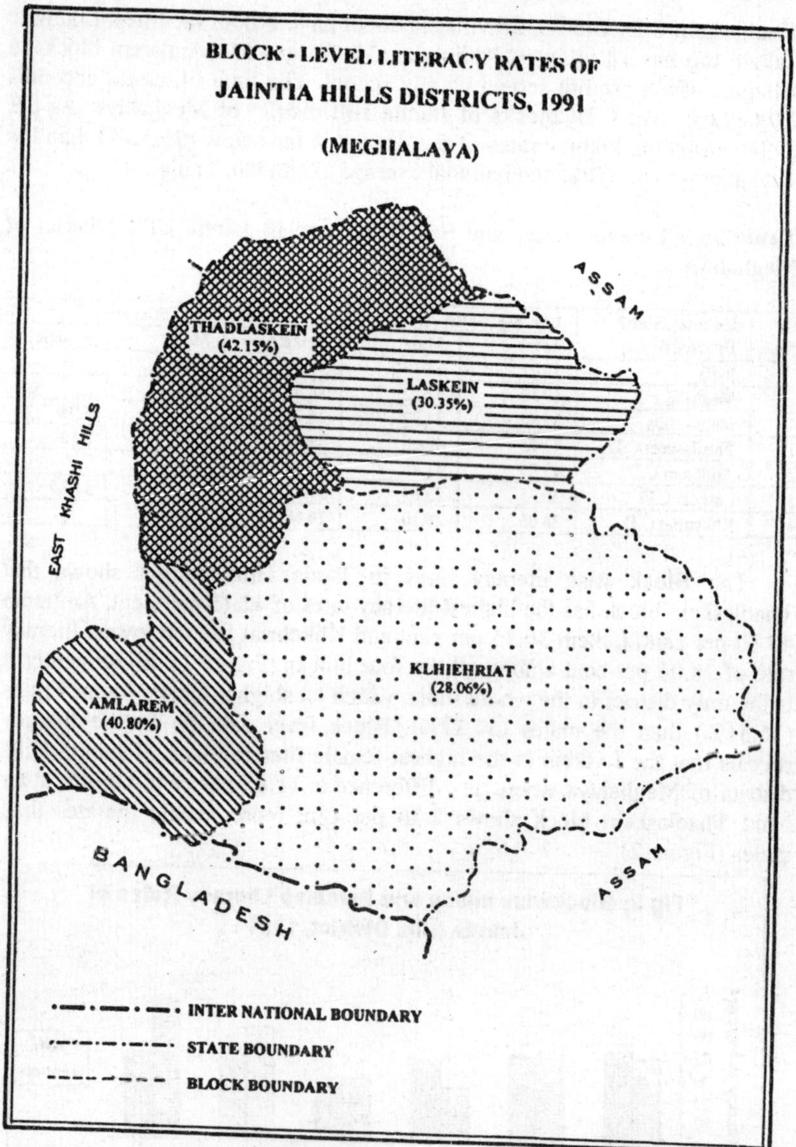

Fig. 16 : **Block level literacy rates of Jaintia Hills District 1991**

TOTAL LITERACY CAMPAIGN

Education is a basic need and an essential infrastructure for the development of human resources of country. Therefore, Govenrment of India is committed to make all out efforts towards achieving education for all by the turn of the century. The National Literacy Mission feels that literacy is an important input in the overall development of individuals. Hence, the Mission has launched the Tottal Literacy Campaign (TLC) through out the country to eradicate illiteracy. With this motive, the Government at Central, State as well as district levels, the TLC project are taken up by the District level government authorities in the different parts of the State. To make people literates and to create awareness of various programmes (sanitaiton, drinking water, eradication of social evils, superstitions, health-hygiene, birth-control, AIDS, women empowerment, conservation of natural resources, heritage and cultural tradition etc.). The State Resource Centre (SRC) of NEHU, with district council authority has organised many programmes in different districts of Meghalaya. Keeping these objectives of TLC in mind, the Jaintia Hills District Literacy Council (JHDLC), Jowai, formulated the TLC project in March 1995 with the Mission to eradicate illiteracy among the people in the age-group of 9 to 45 years. A host of associated objectives of the Council, notably provision of education to the deprived sections of the society through formal and non-formal educational system, improvement of economic standards of various sections of society and awareness of ecological parameters and proper use of natural resources of the district are also incorporated in the TLC project.[7] The TLC was launched in 147 villages covering ony 17.47 percent illiteates till this study. The target learners of Jaintia Hills distric is 57,386 (males 26,484 and females 30,902). As per thedistrict TLC report, the total enrolment number of learners are 32,547 till October 1999 with male 20,453 and female 12,094. These learners are termed as neo-literates which covered 9 to 45 years of age group. The study materials of neo-literates are upplied by State Resource Centre (SRC) NEHU. These materials are called Improved Pace Content Learning (IPCL). Among the total learners, 2,955 have completed level I, level II has been completed by 2,150 learners, and 23,086 learners have completed level III till date.[8] To accelerate literacy drive in jaintia Hills district some non-formal educational institutions, voluntary organisations and NGOs are also involved in the TLC programme. The existing centres of Rural Functional Literacy Project (RFLP), State Adult Education proejct (SAEP), Anganwadis Mahila Samities and other voluntary organisations are also working to promote literacy rates in the district.

CONCLUSION AND SUGGESTIONS

There are immense challenges yet to be met and enormous amount of hard work lies ahead to make the people 100 per cent liteates. Though Total Literacy Campaign has creaed an over all awareness in educaton and development of the district, it is long way to do some much work to achieve the goal. This study indicates that 95 Villages of Jaintia Hills district do not have even primary schools. Therefore, concerned authorities should look into the matter and establish at least one school in each village. On the other hand the adult illiterates should acquire the facilities rendered by different organisations, so that the Jaintia hills District can achieve a satisfactory level of literacy target.

REFERENCES

1. Chattopadhayaa, S. K. (1988), "The Jaintias".
2. Pakem, B. ( ), "The Socio-Political system of Jaintia Tribes of Assam : Analysis of Community and Change."
3. Bareh, H. (1967), "The History and Culture of the Khasis and Jaintia people".
4. Paul , G. ( ), "The place of *Khadduh*- the youngest daughter in Khasi and *Synteng* Society", *Vanyajati,* Vol. IV.
5. Dutta, P. N. (1982), "Impact of the West on the Khasi and Jaintia".
6. Bareh, H. (1996), "Progress of Education Meghalaya".
7. Laso, B. L., & S. Singh (1998), "Concurrent Evaluation Reprot on Total Literacy Campaign in Jaintia Hill District".
8. Directorate of Elementary and Mass Education, Meghalaya, (A report), 1999.

20

FORMATION OF THE JAINTIA HILLS AUTONOMOUS DISTRICT COUNCIL

E. Jyrwa

After India achieved its independence, there was a strong feeling among the tribal people in he hill areas of Assam for regional autonomy and better status within the framework of the Constitution of India. The interim Government of India set up in 1947 also realised the critical situation and aspiration of the hill areas of Assam and wanted to look into the grievances and affairs of the tribal people, so that they might be able to participate in decision making processes and the institutions according to their own genius. At the same time it was realised that these areas require a special type of government and some amount of protection against exploitation by the more advanced people of the plains.

In pursuance of paragraph 20 of the Cabinet Mission's Statement of May 16, 1946 an Advisory Committee was constituted by the Constituent Assembly of India on January 24, 1947. The Advisory Committee in its meeting held on February 27, 1947 constituted two Sub-committees in pursuance of paragraph 19 (iv) and paragraph 20 of the Cabinet Mission's Statement of May 16, 1946. One of the Sub-Committees under the Chairmanship of Shri Gopinath Bordoloi was known as the North-East Frontier (Assam) Tribal and Excluded Areas Sub-Committees. When the Bordoloi Sub-Committee studied the problems of the tribal people it realised that these areas needed protection and safeguards so that they might preserved their way of life and at the same time participates in the political life of the country along with others.

The Bordoloi Sub-Committee recommended an administrative set-up for administration of the hill areas based on the concept of regional autonomy in all matters affecting their customs, laws of inheritance, administration of justice, land, forest, etc. Eventually the Bordoloi Sub-Committee made certain recommendations, the majority of which were to be subsequently included in the Sixth Schedule to the Constitution of India.

The Advisory Committee discussed the Bordoloi Sub-Committees' recommendation thoroughly and accepted most of its recommendations for the administration of Assam relating to the formation of the District

Councils and Regional Councils. The recommendations were accepted with certain modifications which concerned mainly with the classification of the areas, administrative areas, strength of the Council, formation of constituencies for major tribes within the autonomous district fund, control of mines and minerals within the district, application of Union and State laws to the autonomous areas, maintenance of financial accounts, appointment of the Commission to find out the process made by the District Councils and control of the District Councils by the Governor.

The Drafting Committee submitted the Draft Constitution to the President of the Constituent Assembly on 21 February 1948. On 4 October, 1948 Dr. Ambedkar introduced the Draft Constitution and moved that it be taken for consideration. Dr. Ambedkar, in course of his speech, referred to the report of the Advisory Committee on Tribal Areas which came too late to be considered by the Constituent Assembly. Acting on the earlier suggestion of the Advisory Committee made on 7 December, 1947 the Drafting Committee incorporated in the Draft Constitution provisions on the basis of the recommendations contained in the report of the Sub-Committee constituted by the Advisory Committee.

The Sixth Schedule was taken up for consideration in the "first" Second Reading on the 5th, 6th and 7th September 1949. There was a strong protest when the Sixth Schedule was taken up for discussion on September 5-6, 1949. Kuladhar Chaliha saw in the schedule that the British mind is still there. "There is old separatist tendency and you want to keep them away from us". Brajeswar Prasad of Bihar said that he "could not be party to dividing Assam", nor was he willing to jeopardise the interest of India at "the alter of the tribals". Rohini Kumar Choudhury said : "We want to assimilate the tribal people. We were never given the opportunity so far". Prof. Shibban Lal Saksena said that, he had no objection to the establishment of the District Councils, but provision should be made for the absorption of the areas in the province of Assam. There were also some representatives like L. Sahu, A.V. Thakkar, Jaipal Singh, Gopinath Bordoloi and Rev. J.J.M. Nichols-Roy who strongly supported the Sixth Schedule. The Second Reading of the Draft Constitution was completed on 17 October 1949.

The Third Reading of the Constitution as a whole was taken up on 17 November 1949. The Draft Constitution as finalised by the Constituent Assembly on 26 November 1949 was passed and adjourned till 24 January 1950.

Immediately, after the Constitution was brought into force, the District Council comprising of the elected Representatives could not be constituted. Therefore, in the first instance the Tribal Advisory Committees were established in all the hill districts. Accordingly, the Government set up an Advisory Councils. Though the Advisory Councils had no statutory basis, they were only provisional district councils. The Advisory Council for the United Khasi-Jaintia Hills District was inaugurated by the Chief Minister of

Assam, Shri Gopinath Bordoloi at the Government House, Shillong on May 24, 1950.

With the coming into force of the Sixth Schedule to the Constitution of India, steps were taken to constitute District Councils in all autonomous Districts of Assam. Accordingly, the Government of Assam made rules namely, the Assam Autonomous District (Constitution of the District Councils) Rules, 1951 for the Constitution of the District Councils and for the procedure and conduct of business of these district councils and steps were taken for the holding of the first election to the District Council on the basis of adult suffrage. In 1952, the District Councils were constituted in all the districts except in the Naga Hills District. The first elections to all other district councils were held during April-June 1952.

The United Khasi-Jaintia Hills Autonomous District Council came into existence on 27 June 1952. The Autonomous District Council of the United Khasi-Jaintia Hills was formally inaugurated by the Governor of Assam, Jairamdas Daulatram at the Dinam Hall, Jaiaw, Shillong on 27 June 1952. Many things took place in the United Khasi-Jaintia Hills after the Sixth Schedule was introduced in 1952. Right from the inauguration day, on 27 June 1952, a bitter seed of protest against certain provisions of the Sixth Schedule was sown. The inauguration day was a gloomy day for the public of Shillong. There was a big student and youth demonstration against the principle of nomination. This political consciousness among the people immediately flare up when the people carried black flags to protest the principle of nomination. Of course, the protest was not directed against the introduction of the District Council, but it was against the Assam Government's policy in trying to impose the "nomination" of three non-tribal persons as members of the District Council from among the three communities which have nothing to do with the District Council affairs.

Over a period of years it was the experience of the hill people that their hopes were denied. Being disillusioned and frustrated they found no other alternative than to demand the creation of the separate hill state to determine their future according to their own genius.

During the early years of a moment for a separate hill state, the Assam Government was trying to meet the demands of the Jaintia people for special treatment. Hence, five years after the formation of the United Khasi-Jaintia Hills Autonomous District Council on 27 June 1952, some leading representatives to the United Khasi-Jaintia Hills Autonomous District Council from Jowai Sub-division felt that no progress was being made in the direction of uniform administration throughout the Jaintia Hills district by the District Council. As a result, there was a strong move for a separate District Council in the Jowai sub-division. Now let us find out what are the causes and factors responsible for the bifurcation of the United Khasi-Jaintia Hills Autonomous District Council into the Khasi Hills and Jaintia Hills Autonomous District Councils.

When the Khasi and Jaintia Hills were constituted under one administrative unit, the two areas were administered under one revenue district and also under one United Autonomous District Council. However, the Jaintias had their king since long and even when they were annexed by the British, they had their own administrative arrangement. After annexation, the Jaintia Hills with British, the villages in the Khasi Hills were administered directly by the British Government, while the Khasi States were allowed internal autonomy subject to general control of the British Government. The *Dollois* and *Sirdars* in the Jaintia Hills were given judicial powers in addition to their being agents for collection of revenue. They were also expected to undertake ordinary duties of police and to arrest all criminals and repress all disorders within their respective jurisdictions. A *Dolloi* could be empowered by the Deputy Commissioner to dispose cases of person charged for any offence. In the Khasi States the Chief enjoyed civil and criminal powers under the Deputy Commissioner, Khasi and Jaintia Hills. Their powers, however, were higher than those of the *Dollois*. Besides these judicial powers, the Khasi Chiefs functioned as semi-independent rulers and the people being with the *Syiemship* did not pay any land revenue or house tax. In the Jaintia Hills the British Government claimed rights to the raj lands as successor to the Jaintia Kings. But in the Khasi States, the control over land vests mainly with the people where the Khasi Chiefs could claim no right of their own except in respect of lands reserved for the support of the *Syiems*.

At the time when the Bordoloi Committee was examining the future administrative set-up of the tribal areas of Assam, there was a demand from some Jaintias, for keeping the Jaintia Hills separate from the Khasi States. Accordingly, on 1st November 1957, a memorandum was submitted to Shri Govind Ballabh Pant, the Union Home Minister by the members of the District Council and others representing the people of the Jaintia Hills from the Jowai sub-division of the United Khasi-Jaintia Hills District Council on various grounds asking for a separate District Council for Jowai Sub-division and failing this, they expressed their desire for the Jowai sub-division to the centrally administered. The memorandum stated, among other things, that on such maladies was the imposition of a dual taxation, for example payment of land revenue and house tax.

In the meantime the memorandum also stated that from what they had experienced in the past five years, they found that a uniform administration was not feasible. They stated that all lands in the Jowai sub-division were under the control and management of the District Council, whereas, in the Shillong sub-division lands were either the private properties of the so-called *Ri-Kynti* land owners or were held under the control of the Chief and their durbar. In spite of all these differences, the memorandum pointed out one more defect that the District Council could not make any progress in administering the affairs of the district as in the other District Councils like the Garo Hills and the Lushai (Mizo) Hills. One of the reasons that is apparently clear was the presence of diversity in social, economic and political position prevailing in the two sub-divisions.

Another memorandum was submitted to the Prime Minister, Jawaharlal Nehru, on 30th December 1957. In the memorandum, members of the District Council and others from Jowai sub-division had demanded for the creation of a separate District Council for the Jowai sub-division. The memorandum pointed out the advantages of having a separate District Council for the Jowai sub-division and the disadvantages of remaining in the United Khasi-Jaintia Hills District Council. The disadvantages as pointed out by the members was that out of 24 members in the Council, one six members represented the Jowai sub-division in the Council and six other members were nominated from areas other than Jaintia Hills. These members felt that the interest and welfare of the people of the Jowai sub-division were placed at the mercy of the majority members of the Shillong sub-division. Because of this position they felt that the arrangement had created disuniformity in running the affairs of the people. On the other hand, the advantage of having a separate District Council as pointed out in the memorandum was that it would remove the sense of "slavery and inferiority complex" that was lingering in the minds of the Jaintia people. The memorandum pointed out that in a separate District Council of their own, the Jaintia people will have the sense of having the right to govern themselves.

Apart from the memoranda submitted to the Prime Minister and the Union Home Minister, the demand for a separate District Council was repeatedly pursued in the United Khasi-Jaintia Hills District Council by Mr. H. Hadem, the member from Jaintia Hills and at one time an Executive Member of the District Council. On 7th August 1958, Mr. Hadem moved a resolution for the formation of a separate District Council for the Jowai sub-division during the council session. Mr. Hadem was of the opinion that a separate District Council was necessary for the Jowai sub-division in view of the difference in the system of administration prevailing in the Jowai sub-division and requested the Governor of Assam to take steps for its creation. After hearing the views and opinions from all the members of the Council, the Chairman of the Council put the motion moved by Mr. Hadem to vote by raising of hands. 13 members voted against the motion and five members supported the motion Thus the resolution moved by Mr. Hadem was lost by 13 to five votes. The resolution was supported by five of the six MDCs from the Jowai sub-division.

Subsequently, another resolution was brought by Mr. Hadem in 1959 in the District Council reiterated the demand for a separate District Council for the Jowai sub-division. In this council session also, the same five MDCs voted for it. While one member from Jaintia Hills apparently did not take part in the voting as his name did not appear in the division list.

The same resolution came up in the District Council again in 1961. On this occasion, the six MDCs from Jaintia Hills were equally divided on the issue. However, three members of the council voted for the demand for a separate District Council, whereas another three members opposed it.

On 8 July 1961, the Jaintia Durbar after carefully and closely studying the past nine years and the day-today policies submitted a pertition by the Secretary of the Jaintia Durbar on behalf of the Jaintia Durbar to the Governor of Assam through the Chief Minister of Assam, Shillong, which had unanimously urged upon the Government of Assam and the Government of India, "for the immediate creation of a separate District Council for the Jaintia Hills and there by concede to the long felt and vital needs of the Jaintia people". The Jaintia Durbar had pointed out the differential treatment in the administration by the District Council towards the Jaintia people in the Jowai sub-division.

Because of these repeated representation over a period of six or seven years for the establishment of a separate District Council for the Jowai sub-division. In 1963 a Commission was appointed by the Governor of Assam under Notification No. TAD/Con/21/62/293 dated the 26 August 1963 to examine and report in the matter of creation of a new autonomous District for the Jowai sub-division of the United Khasi-Jaintia Hills Autonomous District by excluding the areas comprising of the Jowai sub-division from the United Khasi-Jaintia Hills Autonomous District. The Commission was known as the "United Khasi-Jaintia Hills Autonomous District Commission", under the Chairmanship of G.P. Garman, a retired Commissioner.

The Commission, after its examination and hearing through interviews and also through different memoranda, in its report felt that most historical works agreed that the Khasi and Jaintias were both Mon-Khmer in origin. Therefore, the Commission had stated that historical references were not conclusive as to whether the Khasis and Jaintias were two different tribes. The Commission though that the factor governing the change in attitude were political expediency rather than any conviction. Thus the commission adhered its findings to historical data. The commission found that the general feeling of the protagonist of a separate District Council was that the exemption of a house tax was only a maneuver on the part of the District Council to allay the agitation for a separate District Council for Jowai sub-division and that the United Khasi-Jaintia Hills Autonomous District Council had forfeited their confidence. The Commission appreciated that the difficulties of the District Council were part of a legacy from British regime, and so were the taxes that were prevailing in the Jaintia Hills.

As a matter of fact, the Commission felt that if the inhabitants of Jaintia Hills worked together and maintained the existing system of administration, there was no reason why a separate District Council for Jaintia Hills should not be a success. The Commission thought that the establishment of a separate District Council would, resolve the prevailing tension and bitterness, due to lack of uniformity in administration between them and the Khasis and at the same time the Commission hoped that the separation would lead to a better understanding between them. Accordingly, the Commission recommended the creation of a new Autonomous District Council for the Jowai sub-division of the United Khasi-Jaintia Hills Autonomous District by excluding the areas comprising the areas of the Jowai sub-division from the United Khasi-Jaintia Hills Autonomous District. The Commission however, admitted that there was no good grounds to couclude that the people of the Jowai sub-division and the Shillong sub-division of the United Khasi-Jaintia Hills District belonged to two separate communities. Thus, considering the administrative convenience, the Commission recommended the creation of a separate Autonomous District.

The Commission made its report to the Government of Assam on 24 January 1964. The Council considered the report at its meeting on the 28 April 1964, and decided to accept the recommendations of the Commission. After the report was placed before the Assam Legislative Assembly on 7 and 8 September 1964, the members of the Assembly accepted the recommendation of the Commission in the form of a resolution on a private member's resolution. After a careful consideration of the report, the Assembly passed a resolution approving of the action proposed to be taken by the Government of Assam on the report in question on 8 October 1964.

Accordingly, on the 23 November 1964, a Notification No. TAD/R/50/64 was issued by the Governor of Assam in accordance with the memorandum, which had been placed before the Legislative Assembly of Assam. By this Notification, the Governor of Assam was pleased, "to create a new Autonomous District to be called the Jowai District by excluding the Jowai sub-division of the United Khasi-Jaintia Hills District with effect from 1st December 1964, and that the boundaries of the Jowai District shall be the boundaries of the Jowai sub-division of the United Khasi-Jaintia Hills District".

Meanwhile, Mr. Edwingson Bareh, the CEM of the United Khasi Jaintia Hills Autonomous District Council filed a case in the High Court challenging the validity of the above mentioned notification. The case went up to the Supreme Court, and the court upheld the validity of the Notification. Subsequently, on 1 February 1966, a new Autonomous District Council was established for the Jowai sub-division styled as the Jowai (Latter on Jaintia Hills) Autonomous District Council.

Accordingly, Mr. Edwingson Bareh who was the CEM of the United Khasi-Jaintia Hills Autonomous District Council since March 1963, ceased to be the CEM of the United Khasi-Jaintia Hills Autonomous District Council to become the CEM of the Jaintia Hills Autonomous District Council. The Governor empowered the two Executive Members of Mr. Bareh in the council to continue in office till the appointment of a regular CEM. Mr. Wilson Reade was elected as the new CEM on 7 January 1966. Mr. Wilson Reade retained all the colleagues of Mr. Edwingson Bareh and continues in office till the next election held in 1967.

In fact, the term of the United Khasi-Jaintia Hills Autonomous District Council expired in January 1963. Elections to the Council could not be held in due time and it had to be extended up to 1967.

REFERENCES

1. *Constituent Assembly Debates*, Vol. VIII; Vol IX, Vol XI, (Lok Sabha Secretariat, Parliament House, New Delhi, 1949)
2. Rao, V.V., *A Century of Tribal Politics in North-East India : 1874-1974*, (S. Chand & Co., New Delhi, 1976).
3. Shullai, L.G., *A Brief Note on the Sixth Schedule to the Constitution of India*, (Shullai, L.G. Govt. Press, Shillong, 1988).
4. *Ibid., Noristhan (North-Eastern India) From Union Jack to National Flag*; NERC Special Publication Series 1, (ICSSR-NERC, Shillong, 1994).
5. Government of Assam, *Report of the United Khasi-Jaintia Autonomous District Commission in the matter of creation of a New Autonomous District for the Jowai Sub-division*, (Assam Government Press, Shillong, 1963).
6. "Resolution regarding formation of separate District Council for Jowai sub-division". *Proceedings of the July-August session 1958 of the District Council United Khasi-Jaintia Hills Autonomous District commencing from 30 July, 1958 to 7 August 1958.*
7. Assam Gazette, *Notification* No. TAD/CON/21/62/293 dated 26 August 1963.
8. AIR 1966 Supreme Court 1220 (v 53 c 237) (from Assam : AIR 1966 Assam 1), *Edwingson Bareh, Appellant V. The State of Assam and others, Respondents, dated 29 November 1965.*
9. Assam Gazette, *Extraordinary*, No. 61 (Shillong), *Notification* No. TAD/R/50/64, dated 23 November, 1964.

21

RELEVANCE OF DISTRICT COUNCIL AFTER THE CREATION OF STATEHOOD WITH SPECIAL REFERENCE TO JAINTIA HILLS

S.K. Chattopadhyay

The sixth schedule of the constitution of India was the product of the labor of three person, Sri Gopinath Bordolai, Sri J.J.M. Nichols Roy and Sri B.M. Rau.

Giving the background of the draft sixth schedule, Sri Gopinath Bordoloi said that the corrrect policy, thereof, to remove the doubt and integrate the Tribal people in Gandhian way with in the mainstream of Indian Political system, that is, sixth schedule was intended to provide tribal people a separate government for themselves. Each autonomous district is to have district council or regional council with powers to make law on institution of land, forest, agricultural use of channel or water course, regulation of shifting cultivation, establishment of village and town committees, appointment or succession of chief and headman, regulation of social customs including marriage and inheritance of property, trading by Non-tribals etc.

The working of the sixth schedule in Hills areas of Assam was subject to several strains from the beginning. Though the District Council obtained house tax and land revenue from Jaintia Hills in Khasi Hills proper no such collection was made. In 1953, the District Council under its control and all markets under private ownership, syiemship, Dolloiship and sardarship were made to pay half of their revenue to the District Council. By an amendment in 1957 the obligation of payment by all markets other than private ones was abolished. In practice, even these markets pay to the District Council only one-eight of their revenue. But all the Jaintia markets are privately owned and pay 50 percent of their income to the District Council. There are come more issues, which created dissatisfaction in Jaintia Hills. A movement was started by the congress M.L.A. Sri E. Pohsna for bijurication of united Khasi-Jaintia Hills District Council. A commission was set up by Assam Government under the Chairmanship of G.P. Jarman. On the basis of the recommendation of Jarman Commission,

Khasi and Jaintia Hills District Council was split up on February 1966. Thus there are three District Councils in Meghalaya, Khasi Hills, Jaintia Hills, Garo Hills, District Councils.

This paper intend to examine the need of continuance of District Council even after attaining of Hill State for the tribal people of Khasi-Jaintia and Garo people. Agitaition on the issue of official language bill of Assam Govt. and culmination was full statehood comprising Khasi-Jaintia Hills & Garo Hills came into existence in 1972. It was a difficult matter for the Assam Government to agree to the creation of state and they tried their best to avoid granting full fledged statehood to these Hills with in Assam as Shillong being capital of Assam for over a century, there had been a concentration of substantial number of non-tribal population mainly with in Shillong Municipal Area. Now for all practical purposes Meghalaya in purely a Hill state.

STATUS OF DISTRICT COUNCIL PRE AND POST CREATION OF MEGHALAYA

In Mizoram, the District Council was abolished when Mizo Hills District was elevated to the status of union territory on 29th April 1972. In Nagaland or in Arunachal there was no District Council. Mozoram retained District Council for the 3 minority tribes. Now it is to be examined whether District Council with its present status is beneficial for the state or not. The District Council was an important political institution during Assam Govt. The District Council was created for the protection of the tribal from exploitation and for the preservation of their customs and traditions. The constitution of India provided sixth schedule because there were scope of distrust among tribal population of Assam, that they may be exploited by non-tribals in their own land.

Therefore, the District Councils have autonomous status indealing regulations on trading by non-tribals, for the promotion of their welfare, for the preservation of their way of life, tradition and customs. The District Council is to administer according to their own genious. Paragraph 3 of the sixth schedule deals with the subjects in which District Council will have powers to make laws. The subjects are

a) The allotment, occupation or use or the setting apart of land, other than land which is reserve forest.
b) The Management of any forest not being a reserved forest.
c) The regulation of the practice of Jhum or other forms of shifting cultivation.
d) The use of canal or water caurse.
e) The establishment of village or town committee or councils and their power.
f) Any other matter relating to village or town administration, including village or town police and public health and sanitation.

g) The appointment or succession of chief or headman.
h) Inheritance of property.
i) Marriage and Divorec.
j) Social Customs.

Paragraph 4 and 5 of the sixth schedule invested the District councils with the powers to constitute village court or courts and defined their jurisdiction in both territorial and judicial limits.

Paragraph 6 enumerates executive power of District Councils.

Paragraph 8 invested District Councils with Power to assess and collect revenue from lands. The councils shall have the power to levy and collect taxes on lands, buildings, professions, trades, callings, employment, animal vehicles etc.

Paragraph 10, gave District Councils the Power to make regulations for control of money lending and trading by non-tribals.

District councils have executive, legislative and judicial powers with well laid provision that on certain matters, the governor's assent will be required to making certain regulations. There is no two opinion that District Councils under 6th schedule of the constitution was constituted when predominately tribal areas full under a state Government where majority belong to other ethnic group who are more dominant in respect of population, geographical areas etc. On the same ground, in Tripura, District Councils under 6th schedule are constituted. The sixth schedule contained code for the governance of tribal areas. Sri M. Hidayatulla, former Chief Justice of India commented that the sixth schedule is a very elaborate piece of legislation and its has undergone many changes since it was enacted. Sri Hidayatullah further stated that the provisions of the sixth schedule are hardly a code, they are constitution with in a constitution.

There are provisions of election of M.D.C. for the term of 5 years. All political parties take part in the election with the intention to be party in power in district council. Gradually, the District Council Politics has taken more or less same situation as in the State politics. Let us take the example of present situation in Jaintia Hills District Council. On 21st March 2000, Sri Obil Kyndiat resigned as C.E.M. who was heading a coalition executive council comprising of N.C.P., U.D.P., MDCS expelled from congress. From April 1st Governor assumed to himself all the functions and power of the District Council. Since then, political maneuvering has been going on for formation of Executive Council. Anti defection law is not applicable in District Council. On April 13, like Jaintia Hills, the Garo Hills District Council also brought under the administration of Deputy Commissioner, Going through the process of trial of strength in the Garo Hills District Council over trust vote, it is not difficult to find the practice of horse trading in District Council Politics. Party in Power in the State are in a position to manipulate in this horse trading practice. According to Sri Joh Deng Phormen, an important political leader of the state, District Council will provide opportunities for training in practical politics to budding politicians. There is huge expenditure involved in holding District Council lection. After creation of statehood, situation is thoroughly changed. The party in power in the State Government will always desire to have their own party man in power in the District Council also. There have been lot of tension on this account. Even now, the executive members are having lot of executive powers. There have been huge expenditure in maintenance of perks towards executive member & chief executive member. Moreover, establishment cost is quite heavy. They depend on Govt., grant inspite of sharing taxes in many subjects and having resources exclusively from minerals, forests markets etc. The Jowai District Council has officers an staff numbering around 968 as per detail given below :

S.No.	Category	No. of Post
1.	General Administration	177
2.	Finance & Accounts Department	26
3.	Revenue Department	122
4.	Land Reform Department	12
5.	Taxation Department	38
6.	Forest Department	145
7.	Political Department	23
8.	Civil Work Department	90
9.	Education Department	127
10.	Town Committee Affair Department	32
11.	Judicial Department	48
12.	Legislative Department	49
13.	Stationer & Printing Department	7
14.	Agriculture, Soil, Fishcries & Market	49
15.	Publicity Department	6
16.	Planning Department	17
	Total	**968**

(Excluding Chairman, Vice Chairman etc.)

The current budget outlay for Jaintia Hills District is Rs.15,11,94000.00. Because of disproportionate overhead cost, the Dist. Councils could not retain primary education with them. There were agitation after agitation from primary school teachers all over the state. Ultimately Government took over primary education from District Councils.

CONTRADICTIONS

The District Councils have their jurisdiction in their respective Districts. In case of Khasi Hills Districts the areas comprised with in the municipality of Shillong are excluded from its jurisdiction as per para 20 of the schedule The exclusion of Shillong Municipal Area has been a bone of contention for the District Council. Assam High Court in the case of District Council Vs Drepsila Lyngdoh, gave verdict that only three wards of Shillong municipality viz. European ward, Police Bazar and Jail Road can be excluded. But there is no amendment of Para 20 of the 6th schedule till today.

When the British assumed sovereighty of the Khasi Hills, Indigenous Institutions were not swept away. There were Policy of non-interference over Traditional Institutions. British recognised the Khasi Syiems, Dollois of Jaintia Hills and their authority. Now all these institutions are elected to their office by an election of electoral college, but they are appointed by the District Councils. During British rule the Local Chiefs were under the control of supervision of Deputy Commissioner, but now they are under the control of District Council, i.e. Local Institutions are under the control of Local Self Government, which create problems very often.

The District Councils have Power to appoint and even power to dismiss Local chief. The Indigenous Institutions are also custodian of tradition, culture etc. Even Khasi Syiems has its own judicial system for time immemorial. District Council also has Judicial court and court has been functioning with their appointed judges.

SHOULD DISTRICT COUNCIL WITH ITS POSITION CONTINUE IN MEGHALAYA?

There have been academic discussion regarding utility of District Councils in its existing form after statehood was granted to the people to run their administration according to their own genius. The finance requirement of maintenance of District Council with all its overhead cost is also a matter to be taken into consideration in view of resource constraint of the Government. The revenue of State Government is very limited to carry out the development activities of the State. The District Councils are increasingly facing financial crisis specially after the drying out of resources from timber as restriction imposed on cutting of trees by Supreme Court. The State Government very often has to share its limited resources for recurring District Council for payment of salaries to the staff. At the moment the position of District Council is parallel to State Government in its own jurisdiction. It is not just a local Self-Government as we understand in the Plains with Zilla parrishad, Gaon panchayat. Only modification in its original powers was made by incorporating paragraph 12 A in section 74 of the Assam re-organisation (Meghalaya Act 1969) which provided overriding power with the state legislative over District Council. Under this provision, law made by the state legislative will prevail over any law of the District Council.

On close scrutiny, it will reveal that there are overlapping in the powers and functions of the District Council and the State Government. The District Council which had its utility when the area was under the jurisdiction of the state of Assam and after formation of statehood of

Meghalaya comprising the land and people which had been with Assam created completely different situation. Now, the affairs of Governance is with the democratically elected representatives of the people of Meghalaya.

Out of 60 legislative constituencies, 55 constituencies are reserved for indigenous people. There is no fear of interference of other people in the affairs of tribal people. Moreover, the state Government has better infrastructure. It has well built Government machinery's left by Assam with well-trained manpower to run the administration. The state is in a position to protect the sight of the tribal people, their tradition, land, culture etc., which was one of the considerations for the creation of District Council under sixth schedule Part – A. Areas of the constitution no longer found necessary.

It is felt that after creation of Statehood, District Council may serve the people as local seld government in true sense of the term. It has grass root level contact. The smallness of the constituencies give ample scople for M.D.C.S. to be thoroughly acquainted with their area. District Council will be in a position to carry out development works as would be entrusted by the State Government as well by Central Government. There is now provision of direct funding to local self Government by the central Government. But the existing status of District Councils is in the way to avail of direct funding from central coffer as District Council are more or less constitutionally having autonomous Status. The relationship of District Council and State Government is not interdependent as it should be for the co-ordinated effort of the Government. The parallelism of the set up of the District Council and to that of State Government will not give benefit to the people. At present, there is lack of co-ordination in the functioning of the District Council and the State Government. The District Council may function as an agent of the State Government in development activities. For all practical purposes, the status of the District Council may be framed in analogy top Zilla Parrisad of the local self Government with modification to suit the need of the State and people. After creation of Meghalaya it is felt that the powers viz. Land, forest, judicial may remain with state Government.

The matter of changing of Status of District Council is probably a difficult proposition. A politician when defeated in the Assembly election, try to take refuge as M.D.C. There is no reservation of seats for women as it is there as per amendment of constitution in Local self Government. For modification of the Status of District Council, Public opinion will required to be created for the interest of the people and the State. It will depend on people themselves to create the awareness for the change. There are people now raising their voice. Sri Michqael N. Syiem, secretary, Mait Shaprang, a non-government organisation, has stated in its paper "self interest of Political aspirants need to be sacrificed for the sake of overall development of the state".

REFERENCE

1. Report of the United Khasi Jaintia Autonomous District Commission Shillong – 1964.
2. Syiem N. Michael, "Do we still need the District Council" a paper published by Mait Shaphrang Publication.
3. Phira J.M. 'The Autonomous District Councils of Meghalaya' Kamala Arts Press – 1993.
4. District Plan 1974-75. Jowai – 1974.
5. Shillong Times 'Daily Newspaper', Shillong, S\Dt. 25/03/2000, 02/05/2000 etc.
6. Detail estimate of revenue and expenditure 2000-2001. Jaintia Hills Autonomous District Council Publication.

22

AN APPROACH TO THE ECONOMIC DEVELOPMENT OF JAINTIA HILLS

Susmita Priyadarshini

Jaintia Hill is the eastern most district of Meghalaya with unique physical-ecological, social and cultural diversity. But we cannot say that it is the most developed district of Meghalaya or North-East. There are many factors, which hinder the economic development of this district. Development of any region depends on the capacity to solve three broad categories of problem. This is true for Jaintia hills also, they are

a) Infrastructural problems comprising power transport communication, irrigation etc.
b) Problems related to social services including education, health, drinking water supply and general and economic service.
c) Production problems related to agriculture, animal husbandry, dairy, fishing, horticulture, forestry and industry.

In this paper, I have not attempted to list and discuss all the constraints of economic development. Most of the physical constraints are deleburately left out because they can be easily tackled with given political will and right policy and partly because they are well known. This paper is an attempt to draw the attention of the policy makers as well as the people to certain aspects which have long been ignored.

1. ATTITUDINAL CHANGE

It is the demand of the time to change the attitude of the policy makers as well as the people to a more rational and modern outlook.

a) There is a vague pride in the minds of the Jaintia people that they are rich in natural resources. But man is a part of nature. If one part of nature (people) is poor, inefficient, and backward how can the district/state became rich in natural resources.
b) It is true that the Jaintia hills has been experiencing a considerably higher rate of population growth than that of the states average, during

the last few decades. But all the time, we are concerned with the problem of reducing the rate of population growth forgetting that these people can well be utilised to solve this and several other socio-economic problems. Prof. Julian S. Simon rightly pointed out "More people be cause problem but people are the means to solve these problems. The ultimately source is the people, specially skilled, spirited, hopeful young people, who will exert their will and imagination for their own benefit and in doing so, will benefit all of us as well".

c) Another wrong belief is that capacity building should precede economic development. But every new venture has both advantages and disadvantages. If a new road is constructed and through this road, during trafficing and migration increase then it is surely not an advantage. Again, limitation of Kuznet's theory has also been proved everywhere. So, capacity building and its proper utilisation shall go hand inhand.

2. MANPOWER PLANNING

It is mentioned earlier in this paper that the rate of growth of population in Jaintia hills is higher than other districts in Meghalaya. This rapid increase in population has led to the low level of per capita income and high level of unemployment. But one should not forget men are also he wealth, with the proper utilisation of this wealth, even the problem of rapid population growth and unemployment can be solved along with other problems. It is true that universal education can make family planning, a success. As Govt. has already taken measures for achieving this goal, in this paper, an attempt is made to describe how the education system iteself be used to solve the problem of unemployment in Jaintia hills as well as in India. It is now admitted by all that courses of our colleges and universities are not need – based and employment – oriented. Knowledge is the very purpose of education. But along with it, they should acquire sufficient practical and vocational knowledge so that they can earn their living. But in the absence of projection for future requirement of manpower, education system has failed to plan anything or either creating new skills or ensuring that there is no glut in certain discipline in which capacity is existing. The trend is that by shifting the blame of all melodies on population growth, these policy makers easily ignore their own failures and culpability of framing outdated, backward bending and negative policies. UGC has recently adopted certain policies for providing vocational education and my suggestion is that Jaintia hills should take the advantage of those subjects, which will be beneficial for the economic development of Jaintia hills as well as Meghalaya. A detailed discussion is given below: -

UGC has launched the scheme of Career Orientation to Education at the first degree level in 1994-95 in conformity with the National Policy on Education 1986 (revised in 1992). UGC has prepared the list of courses of

58 subjects in which students can be trained for making them more unemployable and capable of exploiting self-employment opportunities. Colleges can introduce one to 3 course out of 58 subject identified by core committee. Colleges of Jaintia hills should take this advantage by choosing those courses, which have the economic requirement for this district as well as Meghalaya. Selection of right type of vocational course is not an easy task. Again, to fix the no. of students to be admitted to each vocational course is another crucial problem. The better thing will be to knew the potential demand for persons in each sector of the district/state, which specific skill will be required in future, what will be the demand in each branch under each sector in the district/state. For this we can take the help of dynamic input-output analysis. The whole process can be termed as manpower planning. Again, we should also take into account unutilised potential of the state and prospects of development on the basis of these. Manpower planning will be much easier if the states take the initiative. A few vocational courses are suggested for Jaintia hills considering the potential and needs of economy –

a) Diary technology
b) Water Management
c) Floriculture
d) Forest and Wildlife Management
e) Computer Application
f) Applied Geology
g) Textile Designing
h) Industrial Chemistry
i) Rural Craft
j) Sail Engineering etc.

3. PHARMACEUTICAL INDUSTRIES

It is well known that tribal people have vast knowledge about medicinal plants and their medicinal use. This is true for Jaintia people also. Disscoria alata, Ghycyrrhiza glabra, Hydnocarpus Kurzij, Lowsonia intermis, Rouvolfia serpentina, Meringa Odeifera, Centella asiastica, Solanum Khasinum, Turmeric, Cinnaman etc. are found in Jaintia hills. On the basis of their medicinal use, many pharmaceutical industries can be set up. Pharmaceutical use of some of them is mentioned below –

a) Dioscoria Alata : Diosgesin is found in the roots of Diosceria. It can be used for the production of contraseptic pills.
b) Glysyrbiza Glabra : Glycyrizine, glycyrizic acid are found in this plant. It is used in the production of medicine for influenza and cough.
c) Rauvolfia Serpentina : Chemicals like Reserpine Amaline Sepentine etc. are found in this plant. It is used in the preparation on of medicine for nervous breakdown.

d) Locusonia Inermis : Lowsonia Inerthis is used for herbal shampoo production.

4. INFORMATION TECHNOLOGY

On the basis of the fact that information revolution has touched every aspects of our life, we can predict that future development in the new millennium will be linked to the development of information technology. During the last 2 decades, we have noticed explosive development of IT – which has totally changed the concept and meaning of communication in the whole world. The type of change that we have noticed has not only made it possible to exchange news and information and store datas in a very fast and instantaneous manner, but at the same time it has its telling effect on economic, social and cultural lives. In this millennium, it will not be possible to develop enterpreneurship without giving due importance to the various needs to IT. They can rightly be called internet – preneur. But in case of Jaintia hills as well as Meghalaya computer application is very limited. It implies the poor development of the knowledge industry in this area. Whatever development has taken place, it is concentrated in Shillong. Even the entire Meghalaya has little share in computer market in N.E. While conducting survey, this writer found that more than 90% of total market for computer is concentrated in Assam. But, if this area legs behind in this race of information revolution, it will imeply isolation of Jaintia Hills from the modern world. But expansion of computer market depends on three things–

a) Customer awareness or consumer consciousness of the people
b) Govt. Policies
c) Companies own policies for market expansion

Customer will demand something if they feel the need for it. They must realise the benefits accruing from Computer, Internet and E-mail. In Andhra Pradesh, farmers also use computer in their farming system, industry and administration all run with the help of computer. So, a multi-pronestrategy is needed for the expansion of the market. They are discussed below :-

On the Part of the Govt. :-

a) Govt. can provide incentive for establishment of Computer assemblying unit. In Jaintia hills there is no air and rail link. Still there is good road transportation system. Govt. can give subsidy or tax incentive for the establishment of assembling units (like Modular Peripherals Ltd. Already established in Kalapahar Industrial Estate in Assam), Jayantia people are hard working industrious energetic and lively. So, govt. can utilise this psychological advantage of the people to attract them to this sector.

b) There is no company branch office in Meghalaya, Zeneth, HCL & DDE ORG have their N.E. branches offices in Assam. If the Govt. and district administration provide some concession and facilities at the initial stage. The companies will be attracted to set up branch offices there. As Jaintia hills is comparatively underdeveloped. Govt. can offer some special facilities to these kind of companies if they open branches in Jaintia hills. Then it will be like killing of two birds with one stone.

c) As only a few people of this district is computer literate. So a subsidised computer course by different Govt. organisations for traders, shoppers, housewives and recognising computer as one of the compulsory subjects at the school level will definitely ensure the supply of required manpower at this sector.

d) Again, computer application should be introduced as one of the vocational courses in the colleges of Jaintia hills.

On the part of the Companies

a) Offering freebics and gifts along with computers.

b) Warranty is given generally for manufacturing defects only and does not include the damage resulting from accidents or negligence use. So, if warranty is extended for a few particular type of incidents it will lead to the vast expansion of market in this backward areas.

NEED FOR AN AGRICULTURAL UNIVERSITY AND VETERINARY COLLEGE

1) The agro climatic condition with wide range of grass land available throughout the year is best suited for rearing of high yielding stock cattle. Efforts should be made in livestock and poultry development. Most of the areas of the State have remain unexplored due to inadequate availability of infrastructure and other inputs. Hence considerable efforts are necessary to improve the stock and educate farmers in the modern husbandry practices so that they may obtain supplementary income and protective food from this income. Schemes like training of personnel in vertinary sciences, and expansion of cattle, piggary and poultry development programme should be intensified. As traditionally Jaintia people are associated with this livestock industry – they will naturally be attracted to its modern developments also. There is no agri university or agri-college in the state. The state has to depend on training facility etc. outside the state. The Basic research in the agri sector is being done by the ICAR, complex for N.E. region. Acute shortage of technical personnel in agri and veterinary is acting as a deterrent in the Jaintia as well as in other districts. Establishment of a agri university and veterinary college will definitely be a welcome step for the economic development of the districts of Meghalaya including Jaintia hills.

5. SETTING UP SOME SPECIFIC INDUSTRIES

a) Colour Industries

Upland areas of Jaintia hills are used for betel nut cultivation. Betelnut and raw betelnuts are used for production of colour to be used in the printing of clothes and production of furniture paints. Considering the abundance of betelnut, Jaintia hills has distinct advantage in this respect. It is noteworthy that several such kinds of industries have been established in Nagaon district of Assam.

b) The oil from Tezpatta (Cinnamon Taranta) available in this district contains 70% to 80% eugenal suitable for preparation of perfuming chemicals. Efforts are to be made to utilise this resource in an effective way.

c) Fruit Processing Industries

Upland areas in Jaintia hills which are in the border of east Pakistan have orchards of oranges, lemons, limes, pin-apples etc. Taking this advantage, fruit processing industries can be easily established here. Pickles are and jams have wider market in the entire N.E. as well as outside India. So, if fruit processing industries are set up, they will not have to bother for the market. Recently, the centre has drawn up enhanced rates of assistance for the development of such Industries. Under this provision, a concessional rate of 4% soft loan will be granted to all food processing units in these areas, with a repayment period of 5 years after a moratorian of 1 year. Besides the ministry also provides 75% assistance on capital cost, extending upto 100% in certain cases to such small units.

d) Cane and Bamboo Industries

Since the beginning of 90's attraction for all kinds of ethnic and tribal traditional items have been seen all over India. Jaintia people can take the advantage of this change as they are always expert in cane and bamboo products.

Jaintia has a good craftsman for various kinds of handicrafts such as baskets, canestrapes, mats, nets, smoking pipes besides black smoothy items for local use. Cane baskets for tea leaves plucking can get ready markets of tea gardens in Assam. As the time is favourable Govt. should make every possible efforts for the development of this industry even providing training for the development of this industry even providing training for skill development. Recently UNDP in collaboration with NEDFI announced a USI'4 million dollar project for setting up a cane and bamboo technology centre in Guwahati. The project exclusively for N.E. would aim at boosting the market of cane and bamboo, found in abundance in the region, by introducing the latest technology and design besides giving the end products international exposers. This project intends to enhance access of crafts people and small entrepreneurs to improve technology and knowledge, thereby promoting employment and income generation. So, if this project comes up, it will be the sure advantage of the Jaintia people who are naturally skilled in this kind of products.

REFERENCES

1. N.C. Sisodia, "Career Orientation to Education", Page 12-17, University News, Vol. 38, No.11
2. Entrepreneurship Development in N.E. D.D. Mai
3. Past Issues of "Competition Master' and "Times of India".

23

BLUE-PRINT FOR ECONOMIC DEVELOPMENT OF JAINTIA HILLS

P.M. Passah

The present Jaintia Hills district is just a remnant of the erstwhile Jaintia Kingdom, which had been subjected to repeated divisions or partitions since the advent of the British in the North-Eastern region. The first partition took place when the British on 15 March 1835, abolished the kingdom and annexed the rich fertile plains of the Jaintia Parganas in the South, mainly to the then Sylhet district and partly to the Cachar district; and those in the north, to the then Nowgong district of Assam. The second partition took place when the North Cachar Hills Subdivision was created and tagged to the said Cachar District[1].

The third partition occurred at the international level on India's independence on 15 August 1947 when the East Pakistan (now Bangladesh) was created. The fourth in the series of repeated partitions of Jaintia Hills occurred in 1951 when the then Government of Assam sliced away a major part of Jaintia Hills (now commonly known as Block I and Block II) and tagged it to the then district of United Mikir and North Cachar Hills newly created in that year without caring for the dissent note made by the only member of the then Assam Legislative Assembly from Jaintia Hills and who was a member of the Committee set up by the Assam Government to enquire into the feasibility of the proposed new district of the United Mikir and North Cachar Hills district.

This paper however deals with the development potentials of the present district of Jaintia Hills created immediately after the formation of the full-fledged State of Meghalaya on 21 January 1972. The Jaintia Hills, one of the oldest subdivisions created by the British Government, was upgraded into a district on 22 February 1972. More than twenty-five years have passed and certainly some signs of developmental achievements could be seen. Still there is a big gap in all developmental sectors between Jaintia Hills and other districts.

THE RESOURCES

The Jaintia Hills district is endowed by nature with copious rainfall, good soil and climatic conditions, rich deposits of minerals, valuable forest resources, abundant water and wind potentials, and scenic beauty spots. Over and above, its people are hard working and gifted with business acumen.

The occurrence of rich coal deposits side by side with limestone deposits is a great boon to those who wish to start any industrial ventures based on these two minerals. The district has also reported deposits of Clay and Sodium Sulphate in fairly good quantities. The district has 5 (five) major north-flowing rivers, namely, Myntang, Umiurem, Waikhyrwi, Mynriang and Kupli, and 4 (four) south-flowing rivers, which are Myngngot, Myntdu, Prang and Lukha. Thus the district possesses vast potentiality for the establishment of mini-hydro electric project at various places in these 9 (nine) rivers. It has also the potentiality of generating power by exploiting the wind resources[2].

The upland region has more flat lands and fairly extensive river valley than the rest of the upland region of Meghalaya. The important valleys are the Sung Valley, the Jowai-North Valley, the Jowai-South Valley, the Litang Valley, the Letein Valley, the Myntang Valley and the Umiurem Valley. There is luxuriant growth of pine trees over the central plateau, but deciduous forests cover the hills in the lower altitudes both in the northern and southern parts of the district[3]. A tremendous scope also exists for the promotion of tourism industry in the district.

DEVELOPMENT POTENTIAL

AGRICULTURE AND ALLIED ACTIVITIES

The various river valleys and flat lands in the district have been fully exploited and utilized for wet paddy cultivation. The cultivation is done with the help of ploughs and bullocks and a network of water channels connected to hill streams and rivers to irrigate the fields. The ploughs have steel blades and the various process of farm operations connected with wet paddy cultivation are not very much different from those traditionally followed in the plains in other parts of India.

The southern part of the district called the *War Jaintia* though mountainous and steepy and unsuitable for paddy cultivation yet the region is favorably suitable for the growth of horticultural crops. The *tezpata* (Cinnamomum tamala) and *pepper* grow extensively well in this part of the district.

The Jaintia Hills is renowned as an important producer of the best quality turmeric, which has been exported abroad.

The evergreen vegetation and the climatic conditions of the district are very favorable for the development of dairy farming and industry. It was in

Jaintia Hills that the British first introduced the high-yielding crossbred stock of dairy cattle, which were later adopted in other parts of the state[4].

The most important tree in the district is *Pine*, which could be scientifically planted and harvested if pin-grove owners could agree to pool their pine-groves together in a cooperative system as done in Sweden. This could enable the pin-grove owners to raise extensive plantation of pines so as to feed and sustain a few mini paper mills or plywood factories and the few existing saw mills in the district[5].

The forests in the district are also the home of various types of animals and birds. The district is notable for a large variety or orchids and a rare botanical species of *pitcher plant*. The *Umlawan Cave*, the longest cave in Asia, is located in the eastern part of Jaintia Hills. There are as many as a dozen caves in the district. Again Jaintia Hills is famous for the biggest collection of *monoliths* located at Nartiang the summer capital of the erstwhile Jaintia kings. A cluster of monoliths is found at several places in the district. There are as many as 21 waterfalls, big and small, many of which can attract tourists. Besides, there are innumerable places of interest in the district, which can be converted into an important playground for the tourists both national and foreign. The district is thus poised with great potentiality for tourism industry.

INDUSTRIES

The two important minerals, namely, coal and limestone, which are available in huge quantities, can be utilized in the manufacture of Portland cement. So far, only one mini cement plant has been established under the name and style of M/s. Jaintia Cements Limited at Umpleng near Latyrke village in the Sutnga elaka. A few more such mini cements are feasible and viable for properly exploiting and utilizing the two rich minerals available in the district. Large market potentials exist by exporting the Portland cement to foreign countries like Bangladesh, Myanmar, and South-East Asian countries besides the home markets in the whole of north-eastern region.

The district possesses vast potentiality for the establishment of mini-hydro electric projects at various places in the major rivers mentioned earlier. The Kupli river has already been tamed and a large-scale hydel power project was constructed and being managed for the supply of power to most states in the north-eastern region by the North-East Electric Power Corporation Ltd. Another major hydel power project has been sanctioned for being constructed at Leshka of the Myntdu River. With a view to opening up the entire district for the benefit of the rural areas, it would be advisable to construct a number of mini-hydel power projects in various parts of the remaining 7 (seven) rivers of the district. The mini-hydro electric projects would not only prove economically viable and eco-friendly, but they could also be scattered all over the district for the industrial development of the rural areas. Again the mini projects not only could save the huge cost required to be invested in big projects but would also facilitate the establishment and expansion of small scale and cottage industries in the villages all over the district. The employment potential of such mini-projects is also very great.

CAPABILITY BUILDING

But before the rich resources of the district are exploited and utilized, capability building should precede. The development of both economic and non-economic infrastructures need to be properly assessed so that both human capability and the capability of the district are strongly built and raised to the level that can properly exploit and utilize its rich natural resources. This is the task that could be achieved only with the support of the politically conscious people of the district. The Jaintia people are industrious and enterprising. They are also traditionally trade-minded in spite of their low literacy. But they do need state support and guidance to enable them to participate in the acceleration of the tempo of economic development of the district. The state has much to do to build and raise the capability of the people and the district itself[6].

It is true that financial allocation to the district has increased from year to year during the last 25 years but where the money has gone is a big question. The total road length has increased over the years but in what conditions these roads are, may be asked by all those who travel in the district. Except for the national Highway-44, which passes through the district, all other roads are not maintained properly leading to a lot of problems for the travelling public. Many bridges, footpaths, health centres, school buildings, water supply connections and other social services have been provided to the people but the story of their maintenance tells us very unhappy news. The fairly good maintenance of the National Highway-44 does not go to the credit of the state but to the people of the Barak Valley, Tripura and Mizoram who constantly make demand for its proper maintenance as the road serves as the life-line to these states. A number of schools and colleges have been established during the last 25 years but the literacy rate of the district is the lowest in the state.

CONCLUSION

In spite of the provision of various services mentioned above, the infrastructure in the district is still too weak to sustain any vigorous programme for its economic development. There are still serious bottlenecks particularly in the field of inter-state transport, power, entrepreneurial manpower and technical manpower and in the field of social services like health and education.

In the absence of railways and waterways, roads are the only means of communication in the district. Besides the National Highway-44 (N.H.-44), which connects it with Shillong, the state capital, *the district needs a few more inter-state National Highways* connecting its district headquarters of

Jowai to the north with *Nagoan* via Khanduli; to the south east with Haflong; and to the east with *Langting* located on the railway line linking Lumding with Haflong – all these three terminating points are situated in Assam. The National Highway-40 connecting Guwahati in Assam with *Dawki*, an important Land Custom Station on the Bangladesh international border, has been decided to be extended upto Jowai. This would greatly facilitate cross border trade between Jaintia Hills and Bangladesh through Dawki, which is going to be developed into one of the four border towns[7] in the north eastern region by the Central Government. But presently, the Dawki-Jowai portion of the extended N.H.-40 is still extremely in a very bad shape. All feeder roads converging on the National Highways-44 and 40 and on the three suggested inter-state Highways should be metalled and properly maintained as all-weathered roads to facilitate trade and commerce within the district.

The condition of power supply and maintenance in the district leave much to be desired. Until the maintenance and distribution of power are bifurcated and administered separately, the power supply condition in the district as in all other districts of the state will not be smooth and efficient so as to encourage industrial and other development works. It will remain so even after the completion of the Leshka Hydel Power Project.

The educational and health services are equally important to produce capable entrepreneurs and leaders in business and commercial sectors. Thus both the human capability and the capability of the district have to be strongly built and raised to the level that can properly exploit and utilize the rich natural resources of the district. It all depends on the state efforts to guide with its suitable development policy for developing the state at the district level. For, unless all districts are uniformly developed industrially, the lopsided development of the state will continue.

REFERENCES

1. W.W. Hunter, A Statistical Account of Assam, Reprinted 1975, *p.173* and *pp.203-4*; H. Bareh, "Khasi-Jaintia State Formation", in Surajit Sinha (Ed.), Tribal Polities and State Systems in Pre-Colonial Eastern and North-Eastern India, (1987) (K.P. Bagchi & Company, Calcutta), *p.270*; S. Endle, The Kacharis, (1910 Reprinted 1990, Delhi), *p.6*.
2. P.M. Passah, "An Economic Vista of Jaintia Hills" in Silver Jubilee (1972-97) Souvenir, Jaintia Hills District.
3. Meghalaya District Gazetteer, Jaintia Hills District, p.8.
4. P.M. Passah, *op. Cit.*
5. *Ibid.*
6. *Ibid.*
7. The other three border towns are *Saturkandi* (Assam), *Moreh* (Manipur) and *Zowkathar* (Mizoram).